Smarter Power

The Key to a Strategic Transatlantic Partnership

Edited by
Aude Jehan and András Simonyi

Center for Transatlantic Relations
Paul H. Nitze School of Advanced International Studies
Johns Hopkins University

Aude Jehan and András Simonyi, eds., *Smarter Power: The Key to a Strategic Transatlantic Partnership*.

Washington, DC: Center for Transatlantic Relations, 2015.

Center for Transatlantic Relations
The Paul H. Nitze School of Advanced International Studies
The Johns Hopkins University
1717 Massachusetts Ave., NW, Suite 525
Washington, DC 20036
Tel: (202) 663-5880
Fax: (202) 663-5879
Email: transatlantic@jhu.edu
http://transatlantic.sais-jhu.edu

ISBN 13: 978-0-9890294-4-5

Cover images: assault rifle photograph © Vartanov Anatoly; olive tree illustration © Kalenik Hanna; guitar photograph © mekCar.

Contents

Part III: Powerful Assets for a Smarter Future

Preface and Acknowledgements

This book is the result of a research project pursued from 2012 to 2014 and featuring the link between power and legitimacy in the European Union (EU) and the United States (US). The contributors the volume seek to:

- Redefine the concept of power, its key notions and tool box;
- Examine EU and US policies as well as practical and institutional challenges, which stand in the way of a true "Smarter Power" approach.

The editors wish to thank the authors for their contribution, their engagement, their time, and their good cheer throughout the project.

We are particularly grateful to Daniel S. Hamilton for his invaluable comments and insights. We would like to thank all our colleagues at the Center for Transatlantic Relations, and especially Miriam Cunningham, for their assistance.

Finally, we would like to thank Peggy Irvine for her commitment while working with us on the many details related to the design and production of the book.

The views expressed by the authors are their own, and do not necessarily represent those of any institution or government. Other views and data sources have been cited, and are appreciated.

Aude Jehan and András Simonyi
Editors

Foreword

Smarter Power in the Transatlantic Relationship

Daniel S. Hamilton

The authors in this volume examine the degree to which various dimensions of power have become more or less important in a world of shifting relative influence among states and diffusion of state power to non-state actors. They identify some trends that are new and others that are newly important. Yet they also acknowledge that some old truths still pertain.

One old truth is that in certain situations military power remains indispensible. Joseph Nye equates the role of force and the centrality of security to oxygen. "Under normal circumstances oxygen is plentiful and we pay it little attention. But once those conditions change and we begin to miss it, we can focus on nothing else."[1]

As we have seen most recently in Afghanistan, Iraq and Syria, however, military force alone is insufficient to win war or sustain peace; other instruments of power must be engaged.

In this context, another old truth is particularly relevant—a vibrant economy remains the foundation of all elements of power.[2] Economic resources not only underpin military power, they underwrite diplomatic capacity and generate attractiveness. Geoeconomics is not replacing geopolitics, yet greater attention is currently being paid to geoeconomics in part because the key stewards of international order, Europe and the United States, are each challenged by rather fundamental economic problems emanating largely from their respective inability to tackle tough political challenges at home, at a time when rising powers are measuring their influence more in economic than in military terms.

What is newly important is that the financial crisis and attendant recession, exacerbated in Europe by the challenges within the euro-

---

[1] Joseph Nye, *The Paradox of American Power* (New York: Oxford University Press, 2002), p. 7.
[2] Joseph Nye, *The Future of Power* (New York: Public Affairs, 2011), p. 80.

zone and in America by extreme political polarization, have damaged the position of the West in the global system. Cyclical economic weakness, longer-term structural challenges, and severe fiscal constraints—all exacerbated by dysfunctional political infighting—have combined to weaken U.S. leverage. Without U.S. fiscal solvency, economic growth, job creation, and some modicum of bipartisan political leadership, the U.S. is unlikely to be a consistent, outward-looking partner. Washington's leverage will be undermined and its ability to harness the full spectrum of its power resources diminished. Similarly, Europe's protracted crisis threatens to drain confidence in European institutions, weaken European popular support for any type of European strategic outreach, and force European decision makers into unpalatable choices, not only between guns and butter, but about the very sustainability of Europe's economic model.

Economic revival at home is also an essential underpinning for continued transatlantic leadership in the wider world, because the normative appeal and continued relevance of the U.S. and European models for others depends heavily on how well they work for their own people. This has important implications for the type of "soft power" resources at the disposal of U.S. and European leaders.

These domestic challenges are particularly important in relation to what Nye calls the transition of power underway among states. Despite its current problems, the United States remains predominant and able to employ a broad spectrum of power resources as no other. And as Andrew Moravcsik has noted, Europeans have been the only others able to exert global influence across the full spectrum of power.[3] Yet European nations, singly and collectively, are increasingly challenged on that score, and Washington is distracted, even as a host of emerging states are growing in influence and power relative to both the United States and Europe.

As this shift of relative power continues, what in the aftermath of the Cold War had been a sense of global convergence around such Western norms as rule-based institutions of collaboration, open non-discriminatory trading rules, the "democratic peace," and the "Wash-

---

[3]Andrew Moravcsik, "Europe: The Quiet Superpower," *French Politics* 7, no. 3 (September-December 2009), pp. 406-407.

ington consensus" on development has drifted toward a broader and more complex global competition of ideas over such issues as multilateralism, the use of force, the rights and responsibilities of state sovereignty, international justice, and alternative models for domestic governance, particularly the relationship between state and market.[4]

Another development that is new, as opposed to newly important, is the diffusion of power away from all states towards non-state actors.[5] This will limit the relative effectiveness of efforts by states to harness their putative power resources unless they engage private actors. In the 1960s, for instance, official development assistance accounted for about 70% of the capital that went to developing nations. Today it represents only about 13% of total investment in these growing markets. Public-private partnerships are critical to more effective diplomatic and development strategies.

These trends—old, new and newly important—challenge the continued effectiveness of the transatlantic relationship. The United States and Europe are each finding the need to be smarter about how they advance their interests, how they wield their power, and how they harness the potential of the their own partnership. This volume offers some insights and recommendations along the way.

---

[4]Giovanni Grevi and Richard Youngs, "What Norms for a New-Order Transatlantic Relationship?" and Bruce W. Jentleson, "Normative Future: A U.S. Perspective," in Daniel Hamilton and Kurt Volker, eds., *Transatlantic 2020: A Tale of Four Futures* (Washington, DC: Center for Transatlantic Relations, 2011).

[5]As Nye notes, "For all the fashionable predictions of China, India, or Brazil surpassing the United States in the next decades, the greater threats may come from modern barbarians and nonstate actors.... Power diffusion may be a greater threat than power transition." *The Future of Power*, p. xii.

Part I

Might Does Not Make Right

Chapter 1

Smarter Power:
A Mindset or the Way Forward?

Aude Jehan

Over the last decade, expensive and unpopular wars, recession, ballooning debt and the rise of China as well as regional powers have underscored the limits of traditional power, or Hard Power, into focus. So far, Smart Power has been understood as the idea that effective foreign policy must rely on a tailored synthesis of both Hard and Soft Power adapted to specific circumstances.

There has been a growing interest in the idea of Smart Power—defined as the effective combination of Hard and Soft Power—in policy circles on both sides of the Atlantic. Nevertheless, academic interest in Smart Power has been lacking. This is surprising given that a significant proportion of scholarly work in international relations deals fundamentally with different forms of power. It is increasingly common for international relations scholars to mention it, but only a few have researched its implications, and even then, almost exclusively in relation to U.S. power.

Hard, Soft and Smart: Defining the Concepts

Scholars have defined "power" as the ability to influence an entity to act in ways in which it would not act otherwise. Hard Power is the capacity to coerce it to do so. Thus, Hard Power strategies focus on military intervention, coercive diplomacy, and economic sanctions to enforce national interests (Campbell and O'Hanlon 2006; Cooper 2004; Wagner 2005).

In contrast to Hard Power, Soft Power is the capacity to persuade others to do what one wants. The concept was introduced by Joseph Nye in 1990, and expanded in his later works. Nye defined it as the ability to get what one wants through persuasion or attraction rather than coercion (Nye 1990). Soft Power creates attraction and encompasses nearly everything other than economic and military power (Cooper 2004). Nye (2004) stated, "In terms of resources, Soft-Power resources are the assets that produce such attraction." Soft Power has become a central analytic concept in foreign policy discussions.

Scholars like Ian Manners, who explore the idea of Europe as a normative power, argue that the more the EU militarizes, the more it will lose its normative power, regardless of the fact that such militarization strengthens the EU's ability to engage in humanitarian action (Manners, 2006). This view supports the notion that on some level, military power is viewed as coercive and decisive. Alexander Wendt refers to this as "rump materialism" (Wendt, 1999). Nonetheless, the fact remains that there are still numerous and significant ways in which military power is attractive. The case of the EU makes this ever more apparent. The same type of argument can be made about some of the most "innocuous" forms of Soft Power, such as public diplomacy, educational exchange, or cultural diplomacy. Their purpose is to encourage engagement, a two-way dialogue, and listening, but they may easily cross the line into propaganda and indoctrination (Cull, 2009).

With these nuances in mind, the overarching argument remains that we cannot associate the tools with the type of power. What is most important is whether the tool is used to coerce or to attract. This is a basic point that sets the stage for a better understanding of Smart Power. It also raises several broader questions. Are Hard and Soft Power just two sides of the same coin? Or, are they in some ways intrinsically different? How are Hard and Soft Power perceived? How are various audiences impacted by the exercise of power? (Davis Cross, 2011)

Smart Power in Practice

Hillary Clinton, while U.S. Secretary of State, used Smart Power to highlight the need for the United States to pull all the levers of power and influence, including its military, diplomatic, cultural, humanitarian, legal, and technological dimensions. She invoked Smart Power as the idea that an effective foreign policy must place principal reliance on a tailored synthesis of Hard and Soft Power adapted to specific circumstances.

Thinking about U.S. constraints on power may not come naturally to policy makers for whom the United States and superpower have long been synonymous. In the aftermath of September 11, the ambition driving President George W. Bush's invasion of Iraq was grand. It was nothing less than the remaking of the entire Middle East. The doubling of the U.S. defense budget within a decade reflected a sense of limitless resources and bespoke of unwavering faith in what could be achieved through their investment from turning Iraq into a friendly democracy and to transforming Afghanistan. Little attention was paid to the interplay of political and military power, the absence of political legitimacy or indigenous support, or to the fact that military outlays may have diminishing returns.

Secretary Clinton used Smart Power to push for increasing resources for diplomacy, more civilian shoes on the ground in Iraq and Afghanistan, enhanced non-military expeditionary capabilities, and more public diplomacy. And she successfully enlisted the Department of Defense to chime in with her, supporting these arguments on the grounds that U.S. foreign policy needs to operate more like a jack knife than a hammer. By explaining why it was smart policy to match military capacity with stronger civilian and diplomatic counterparts, she could argue for the restructuring of American power without being seen as weak on defense (one of the traditional main arguments against additional resources for diplomacy and civilian capacity). Then, part of Smart Power's appeal certainly laid in its expansiveness: the idea of "doing more."

Is Smart Power Over?

In 2014, it seems hard to deny that the wars in Afghanistan and Iraq have exposed the limits of conventional military advantage in waging so called non-traditional warfare. At the same time, non-traditional warfare appears to be becoming ever more the tradition. American influence is also suffering from a less tangible hyper power hangover. U.S. actions are viewed through the lens of decades when its power was overweening and the skepticism is there. Yet, the expense of very large civilian deployments has become difficult to justify. It is now more obvious that there are things that even highly skilled and plentiful teams simply cannot accomplish in difficult places, regardless of how hard they try. In a way, it seems the whole debate has gone full circle. The George W. Bush administration rejected, then embraced it out of perceived necessity and hard-won experience. The Obama Administration embraced it and has now rejected it out of necessity: a hard-won experience of a different sort. The European Union too has tried to embrace it for the last decade but without concrete success.[1]

Despite the fact that the coexistence of Hard and Soft Power has long been observable and still remains extremely accurate, Smart Power seems to have become outmoded. As Davis Cross explained (2011), this is likely because the definition of Smart Power—an effective combination of both Soft and Hard Power—is analytically useless. Since effectiveness is wrapped into the definition, we cannot immediately use the concept to assess the degree to which Smart Power works. "Smart," as an adjective, describes the outcome, and provides no hint as to the process or the alternatives. But there is much to be gained from rethinking Smart Power.

In her 2004 *Foreign Affairs* Smart Power article, Suzanne Nossel compared the global order established by Roosevelt and Truman in the 1940s and 1950s to an electrical grid connecting multiple power sources and grids. The power to contain threats and address problems is spread across a grid of institutions, sovereigns and non-state actors. When the grid works well, the load is spread and no node is overworked or fails. But for the grid to be reliable, the United States and the EU, as well as any other major player[2] need to invest wisely in building it. Sometimes, efficient power also means taking on discrete tasks, as illustrated by the operation in Libya, where the United States

---

[1]According to some scholars, of all the Lisbon Treaty's innovations, the launch of the European External Action Service (EEAS) on December 1, 2010 most demonstrates the EU's commitment to Smart Power. Rather than being responsible for enacting the policies of just one institution, the EEAS should facilitate better coordination of Hard and Soft Power, capitalizes on a successful tradition of professional diplomacy, and amplifies Hard and Soft Power (Davis Cross, 2011). In this sense, the EEAS is set to become the embodiment of common EU foreign policy, and is in the process of cultivating a distinctive institutional identity (Whitman, 2010). But while the potential for effective Smart Power clearly exists, it has not yet enabled the EU to speak with a common voice.

[2]Referring to Smart Power in this chapter, I refer to the general concept of governance as defined in the first paragraph. Then, it is not limited to the United States.

relied heavily on allies and played a decisive and indispensible role but one that was rather narrowly confined.[3]

As this book aims to demonstrate, the discussion regarding Smart Power is not over, but it is not as simple as it appeared originally. Reflecting on the developments of the last decade—such as the budget battles, joblessness, the drains and ambiguities of the Iraq and Afghanistan wars—Smart Power needs to pivot towards sustainability.

A simple step in enhancing the utility of the concept of Smart Power is to take effectiveness out of the definition (Davis Cross, 2011). Smart Power can be redefined as the strategic and simultaneous use of coercion and co-option. Another step in enhancing the utility of Smart Power is to recognize the diverse ways in which Hard and Soft Power can be combined, which builds upon the above analysis of the tools of power. It opens up potential research agendas to consideration of both forms of power in tandem, rather than separately. For example, Smart Power might entail long-term attraction alongside short-term use of coercion when necessary. Long-term Soft Power could involve cultivating legitimate and efficient domestic institutions, maintaining a rapid reaction military force on standby, or projecting elements of domestic culture that have universal appeal. It may also come about through consistent outreach to foreign audiences through public diplomacy efforts, such as support for cultural programs or science diplomacy.[4]

As the next chapters will demonstrate, we certainly should not lose the wider range of tools that are now being deployed more assertively and strategically but we need to make sure that the effort does not leave the toolbox empty. Against that backdrop, the ambition must evolve towards a vision that does not simply deploy more and bigger tools against intractable problems but one that operates selectively to maximize leverage.

---

[3]For more details, see Annemie Neyts-Uytterbroek, *A Smarter Power and the Ability to Influence Behavior*, in this volume, Part II, chapter 7.

[4]For more details, see Tom C. Wang, *Science Diplomacy: Transatlantic Asset and Competition*, in this volume, Part III, chapter 11.

Values Should be a Fourth Avenue to Sustain both EU and U.S. Influence

A rather neglected point in terms of influence is related to the usage of convening power to assertively shape international norms that enforce universal values. President Obama's convening of a Global Nuclear Security Summit in 2010, for example, put the political backing of fifty countries behind a set of commitments to secure vulnerable nuclear material, keeping it away from the hands of terrorists and proliferators.

Convening power can also have a critical preventive effect stopping regressive norms from taking hold. An example lies in the Obama administration's leadership position to bridge differences over how to combat religious intolerance towards Muslims and other groups. Following the explosive emotions that surrounded the Quran burning[5] or the publication of Danish cartoons, there was an effort to adopt a global blasphemy ban, a binding treaty that would combat religious intolerance through prohibitions on speech.

In December 2011, the U.S. State Department thwarted that effort by hosting three days of talks with foreign governments and international organizations, including the Organization of Islamic Cooperation (OIC), on implementing "resolution 16/18," a measure adopted "by consensus"—without a vote—at the U.N. Human Rights Council in March 2010. Critics regarded the measure as an attempt to outlaw

---

[5]In July 2010, Terry Jones, a controversial pastor of the Christian Dove World Outreach Center in Gainesville, Florida, U.S., announced he would burn 200 Qurans on the 2010 anniversary of the September 11 attacks. He gained media coverage, resulting in international outrage over his plans and pleas from world leaders to cancel the event. In early September 2010, Jones cancelled and pledged never to burn a Quran. Jones's threat sparked protests in the Middle East and Asia, in which at least 20 people were killed. In reality, Jones appears to be an obscure bigot with about 50 deluded followers. But in the media, Jones has become the world-famous protagonist of a parable of religious intolerance.

On March 20, 2011, Jones held a "trial of the Quran" in his Gainesville church. Finding the scriptures guilty of "crimes against humanity," he burned it in the church sanctuary. Protesters in the northern Afghanistan city of Mazar-i-Sharif and elsewhere attacked the United Nations Assistance Mission, killing at least 30 people, including at least seven United Nations workers, and injuring at least 150 people. Jones disclaimed any responsibility. Norwegian, Swedish, Nepalese and Romanian nationals were among the UN workers killed. The 4th April 2011 killing of two US soldiers by an Afghan policeman was attributed to anger over the burning of the Quran. American news analysts criticized and blamed Hamid Karzai, president of Afghanistan, for drawing attention to the Quran burning.

valid and critical scrutiny of Islamic teachings, as some OIC states do through controversial blasphemy laws at home. The EU was also concerned that the resolution considered the world as "monolithic religious blocs," while religious hatred was primarily a threat to individual freedoms. Despite those concerns, the resolution, formally entitled "combating intolerance, negative stereotyping and stigmatization of, and discrimination, incitement to violence and violence against persons based on religion or belief," was championed by the administration and endorsed by the full UN General Assembly.[6] This provides a good example of concerted action by states, at both national and international levels and emphasizes the importance of Smart Power.

Both the EU and the U.S. can draw on the gravitational pull of personal freedom and respect for democratic values as part of their attraction. But these should not be cast as American values or European values, but as universal values, enshrined in international instruments.

The emphasis in recent years on putting internet freedom on the human rights agenda, proclaiming LGBT rights as human rights, and making women's rights a centrepiece has positioned both the EU and the U.S. on the side of billions of rights holders worldwide. These kinds of priorities should stay on their agenda, to help them gain more authority, win over more citizens, and advance international norms that will reinforce the spread of democracy and human rights. In addition to being the right thing to do, these efforts build sustainable power.

The core characteristics of the 21st century international system, interconnectedness and the need for cooperation can make achieving durable solutions to difficult problems more challenging. The so-called "Arab Spring" highlighted the risks of loss of moral authority that can result from Western support of repressive regimes. Unlike the peoples of Eastern Europe, who underwent a democratic transition in the 1990s, citizens of Egypt, Yemen, Tunisia, and Syria do not look to Western countries as natural allies or models. Once again, both the

---

[6]Secretary of State Hillary Clinton used the opportunity of the State Department-hosted talks with foreign governments, the OIC and other international bodies to stress the importance of freedom of speech in the United States. She argued that "the best way to treat offensive speech is by people either ignoring it or combating it with good arguments and good speech that overwhelms it." Source: http://cnsnews.com/news/article/un-adopts-religious-intolerance-resolution-championed-obama-administration#sthash.B41Gt7Xd.dpuf (last accessed: June 1st 2014).

EU and the United States have had rather scant influence over the evolution of these countries, despite their historical links or their strategic and economic interests in the region. International aid—provided mainly by the United States and the EU—and backing for the regime in Bahrain or in Syria undercut their credibility as a force for change in the eyes of citizens throughout the region. Just as being for rights can build sustainable power, acting against them can undercut it and drain power and influence away.

In the case of Europe, one of the guiding principles to reinforce its Smart Power should be to project its values and interests in its own neighborhood more effectively. As Olli Rehn already highlighted in 2008—at this time he was the EU Commissioner for Enlargement - this projection of the EU method and model (in enlargement policy) has had a transformative power over decades in numerous countries, from Spain to Poland, from Greece to Estonia. "It needs likewise to be reinforced in the EU's neighborhood policy. I am not advocating a security strategy where "one size fits all". The EU has to use its policy instruments creatively and flexibly. When we seek to promote our values, we need to use different approaches in enlargement, associate, neighborhood and third countries. We can see why this is necessary as we look at the EU's immediate neighborhood in the Southeast and East. We can see that the countries in this region are at different stages in the historical evolution of international relations."[7] I would also argue that today, more than ever, this "transformative power" needs also to be reinforced within the EU itself, in order to bring Europe together politically. Accepting the limits on national power is certainly not easy. It has never been, neither in the United States nor even in the smallest of European countries. The charge of "decline"[8] on both sides of the Atlantic makes it easy to dismiss arguments that address constraints on influence. Simply acknowledging some of these constraints

---

[7]*"Europe's Smart Power in its Region and the World,"* by Olli Rehn, EU Commissioner for Enlargement, Speech at the European Studies Centre, St Antony's College, University of Oxford, May 1, 2008.

[8]Since the late 1980s and the early 1990s, American decline dominated academic discussions. At that time, some of the famous "declinists" were Derek Leebaert, and Samuel Huntington. But even Joseph Nye, who served under Presidents Carter and Clinton, commented that America's "Soft Power—its ability to attract others by the legitimacy of U.S. policies and the values that underlie them—is in decline." In Europe, the economic crisis was seen as the end of the European project. Many "Eurosceptics" and "declinists" stated that the euro was an economic disaster which would turn both the Eurozone and the European Union apart.

can be characterized as capitulating to rivals, as losing confidence or lacking courage. But great leaders, companies, and countries do not stay great by standing still. They see the changes around them and act, distinguishing themselves by how deftly they can retool and capture new opportunities. Lifting the stigma of a candid appraisal on shifting power dynamics can lead the United States and the EU to construct foreign policies that are not only smart, but also sustainable.

Conclusion

Some may mock the idea of sustainable power as a retreat. But as Esther Brimmer comments, "there are those who suggest that multi-lateral engagement is less powerful, I would say exactly the opposite. Smart Power provides more tools, not less. Smart power provides more ways to lead and more ways to gather support. Smart power provides more ways to cooperate and build support from others."[9] Like large companies faced with globalization, new market forces, and obsolete elite legacy systems, both the EU and the United States need to adapt urgently. We often forget that adaptability, historically, is one of the greatest strengths they have in common. Europe had to rein-vent itself constantly throughout history, moving ahead from famines, wars, dictatorships and revolutions. The United States evolved from being a colony to becoming a regional power, one of two super pow-ers, and finally the lone super power. In an era of military and eco-nomic constraints we must draw on that adaptability to reinvent the concept of power once again, as well as the transatlantic partnership. Making power renewable entails several steps. One way to do it is through transparency and more open debates. But the first step is undoubtedly the rebuilding of economic strength to make new invest-ments, and ensuring the support and competence of our own popula-tions. We have been saying this for a few years on both sides of the Atlantic. It is the reason why, in this book, we will focus on elements more squarely in control of foreign policy makers.

---

[9]Assistant Secretary Brimmer's closing speech, *"Smart Power in Action: A View from the Obama Administration,"* during the *Disentangling Smart Power: Interest, Tools and Strategies* conference, organized to launch this research project at CTR, SAIS, Johns Hopkins University, on June 4, 2012.

References

Campbell, Kurt and O'Hanlon, Michael, (2006). *Hard Power: The New Politics of National Security*. New York: Basic Books.

Cooper, Richard N., (2004). "Is 'Economic Power' a Useful and Operational Concept?" Working paper series, 04-02, Weatherhead Center for International Affairs. Harvard University.

Cull, Nicholas J., (2009) "Public Diplomacy: Lessons from the Past," *CPD Perspectives on Public Diplomacy*. USC Center on Public Diplomacy. Los Angeles: Figueroa Press.

Davis Cross, Mai'a K, (2011) "Europe as a Smart Power: The Impact of the European External Action Service," American Political Science Association.

Manners, Ian, (2006) European Union "Normative Power" and the Security Challenge. *European Security*, Vol. 15, No. 4, 2006, pp. 405-421.

Nossel, Susan, (2004) Smart Power. *Foreign Affairs*, Vol. 83, No. 2, pp. 131-142.

Nye, Joseph Jr. (2004). *Soft Power: The Means to Success in World Politics*. Public Affairs. New York.

———. (2008) *The Power to Lead*. New York: Oxford University Press.

———. (2009a) Get Smart: Combining Hard and Soft Power. *Foreign Affairs*. July/August.

———. (2009b) Smart Power. *New Perspectives Quarterly*, Vol. 26, No. 2, pp. 7-9.

Wagner, Christian, (2005), From Hard Power to Soft Power? Ideas, Interaction, Institutions and Images in India's South Asia Policy. Working paper no. 26, *Heidelberg Papers in South Asian and Comparative Politics*, University of Heidelberg.

Wendt, Alexander, (1999) *Social Theory of International Politics*. Cambridge: Cambridge University Press.

Whitman, Richard G., (2010). Strengthening the EU's external representation: the role of the EEAS, Brussels, European Parliament.

Chapter 2

Eliminating the Hard/Soft Power Dichotomy

András Simonyi and Judit Trunkos

The Legacy

During the Cold War, a battle between two major political ideologies—one promoting democracy and freedom, and the other authoritarian rule—took place. Countries on both sides of the battle had an arsenal of tools of Hard Power and what today we call Soft Power. The dichotomous conceptualization of power has been with us for a long time, even if we did not perceive it.

The end of the Cold War led to efforts to rethink the concept of power. Thanks to the pioneering and thought-defining works of Joseph Nye, the concept of Soft Power as a fundamental element of our strategic thinking has taken root. Professor Nye started a revolution in redefining our power resources altogether.

The power toolbox consists of Hard and Soft Power tools, the former being tools of force and domination that are coercive in nature. Traditionally, people conceive of power as Hard Power, which has been used to make others adopt or follow policies that are beneficial to those who possess such power. Hard Power has been used excessively through the centuries. Superiority in war-fighting capabilities gave powers an edge that put them in positions of coercion and domination either by winning wars or by the threats they posed to others.

Soft Power, however, has been part of the power toolbox for centuries too. Throughout history, rulers relied on it to convince and persuade. Soft Power has always accompanied Hard Power. Following wars, the occupying forces often turned to ways to accommodate the material and non-material interests of the occupied. The courts of the Ottoman Empire and Europe used the arts, culture and cuisine to entice, influence and convince the occupied. One could argue that the Catholic Church—with some examples to the contrary (the inqusition)—is a great example of Soft Power. The Vatican has had a disproportionate global influence for more than fifteen hundred years. At times, it forged alliances with rulers, but had only a small army of its own, the Swiss Guard, which never had more than a few hundred members. It wielded enormous political and economic influence even in the most turbulent times. It did that first and foremost by the virtue of Soft Power.

The modern *concept* of Soft Power, and a conscious use of it to advance interests and values, as we understand it today, was born in the 20th century. The idea that persuasion and influence by attraction can be an effective way to advance strategic interests is a relatively new phenomenon. Despite the fact that possession of effective military power is still the single most important element in defining a country's global influence, other elements of power gained prominence. The use of military force to advance global interests remained predominant, but other aspects of "warfare" acquired a prominent role too.

The victory of the ideal of democracy over communism provides the strongest proof of the power of persuasion and attraction. The United States did not win a single "hot" war (except for the invasion of Granada in November 1983) in the second half of the 20th Century. The United States and its allies won, however, the Cold War, in which no shots were fired between the two adversaries represented by NATO and the Warsaw Pact. Arguably, the ability to maintain peace for forty years was very much due to the military power of the West. It won the Cold War by out- arming the Soviet Union. Without its ability to attract, however, without inducing the deep conviction that the free and democratic governance model is superior and more effective to the authoritarian model, the West might not have won the Cold War, and countries like Poland and Hungary might not have broken with the Soviet Empire. Soft Power played an enormous role in changing the course of history, in lifting the iron curtain and bringing down the Berlin Wall.

Unfortunately, the success of the West's Soft Power has been misleading in many ways. It has led some to believe in the superiority of Soft Power over Hard Power. This interpretation is wrong. Without its possession *of effective* Hard Power, the West could not have won the Cold War. It needed both.

As a result of new thinking, which emerged from scholarly circles as a response to the disappearance of the East-West confrontation, it is often wrongly assumed that Soft Power is by definition good and Hard Power is bad. This assumption is false. It was perhaps the result of the elite scurrying to cash in their share of the spoils of change and the efforts to distribute the peace dividend. This thinking may be more prevalent in Europe than in the United Stats but the latter has not been immune to it.

The limits of Soft Power, the way it can and will be used in a world of globalized economy, super-connectivity, social media, and mediums that are yet to be invented, are still unknown. The efforts to compare and quantify different elements of power as better vs. worse or good vs. bad can lead to dangerous simplifications and wrong conclusions. Power has no such qualities. These are moral qualities, which may matter in a philosophical sense, but do not matter in a practical sense. Power can be positive or negative, effective or ineffective, however, at the end of the day, whatever its qualities, it is just power.

Power has been evolving in its dimensions, tool qualities, impact and effectiveness. Whether by attraction and persuasion or by the threat of use, or de facto use of force, power is a means to advance interests and values. Optimally, those interests and values coincide with the interests of the global community. It is optimally positive. Unfortunately, that is rarely the case.

There is another false assumption, namely the idea that Soft Power is per se more effective and less costly. Investigating the cost/impact relationship (on which surprisingly little research has been done thus far) this is simply wrong. If the basis of calculation is cost/benefit, much attention must be paid to both its short-term and long-term effects. The timeframe, within which it is possible to launch various Hard and Soft Power tools, must also be considered in the calculation. The life span of strategic Hard Power tools is longer; most Soft Power tools "age" faster.

Spectral Power

Considering all of the above, it is in our interest to take a new look at power in the 21st century and entertain the question of how we can overcome the dichotomy of Hard and Soft Power. Measuring Hard Power is not a problem. Measuring Soft Power means navigating in uncharted waters. In this chapter, we will discuss methods of measuring Soft Power and make a case for finding better ways of measuring power in its entirety, including the entire spectrum.

In doing so, we will have a better understanding of the nature of power itself, and the way it might evolve in the future. Whatever the result of the research on measuring Soft Power, it can be stated from the outset that the artificial segmentation, the categorization of power tools into Hard and Soft is not necessarily a useful way of economizing our resources. A new conceptualization must be introduced.

Power is *spectral*.[1] The spectral power concept dissolves the rigid borders between Hard and Soft Power. It allows us to look at the power toolbox as a whole, a linear softening from Hard to Soft. It also allows us to have a holistic approach to power. It will help us better plan our assets. It will force us to rethink the way we look at countries and groups of countries in terms of present and future possibilities to shape the world we live in. If it is just power, in its different incarnations, then the power assets can be more easily combined and smaller countries can play a more significant role. Countries big or small will more readily use whatever power they have to advance common, regional or national goals.

No doubt, the battle between big powers will be fought most likely on the economic, trade and cultural fronts, rather than in hot wars. Nevertheless, military capabilities, i.e., the ability to employ Hard Power tools will continue to be a decisive factor in a country's or a group of countries' ranking among the powerful.

The dichotomy of Hard and Soft Power has led to the artificial division of our power tools into two sharply separated groups of tools: hard and soft, whereas a vast array of our tools of power can hardly be categorized that simply. It can be argued that power should rather be seen as linear, progressing from hard to soft—red to blue—with the "brackish" zone in between covering "yellow" and "green." The colors on the spectrum of light change gradually, so does power in its means of delivery

---

[1]The concept of Spectral-Power was first outlined in the joint study by Andras Simonyi and Markos Kounalakis in their study "The Hard Truth about Soft Power," published by the USC Center for Public Diplomacy in August 2011: http://uscpublicdiplomacy.org/sites/uscpublicdiplomacy.org/files/legacy/publications/perspectives/CPDPerspectivesHardTruthAbout-SoftPower.pdf (last accessed: June 1, 2014).

and impact. The hardest tools of power are arguably the strategic military tools. These we would place at the "hot" or "red" end of the power spectrum. The softest tools are the ones of direct personal interactions, cultural diplomacy, youth exchange and the like. These we would place at the other extreme, the "cold" or "blue" end of the spectrum.

Most tools of power do not fit the simple categorization of Hard and Soft Power, "red" and "blue." There are tools of power that are hard in appearance and soft in their impact, and there are ones that are soft in appearance, but hard in their impact. Examples for the first are U.S. militarily-assisted support efforts for the humanitarian mission following the 2013 Typhoon Haiyan disaster in the Philippines as well as after the tsunami in the Indian Ocean in 2004. Without the help of the most sophisticated military vessels, which are hard tools of power, this arguably Soft Power humanitarian action could not have taken place. We therefore categorize it as "Soft-hard", as it needed heavy military organization and equipment to make it happen.

Rock-and-roll music is soft in its appearance yet it had immense influence on millions of people in Eastern Europe, and was of strategic importance in generating and fermenting change. It was hard in its impact. As it prompted (and prompts) regimes that suppress free speech to spend an enormous amount of resources to fight it, we argue that it should be categorized as "Hard-soft."

One wonders where to place the non-military act of NATO enlargement, the Soft Power aspect of which was far more important than the military one. The perspective of membership, the attraction of belonging to the elite defense alliance of the West, was the ultimate tool to entice former Warsaw Pact members to go through difficult reforms. To date, too few recognize the Hard-Soft Power aspects of the NATO enlargement process. Likewise, the act of enlargement of the European Union is a hard soft-power tool, which by the means of attraction has forced candidate countries to make long-term strategic commitments in a vast array of fields.

A gradual scale is necessary to evaluate power tools, and consider their influence based on their strategic and long-term impact, that will alter the balance of power or the attitudes of a country or groups of countries. Power, as we conceptualize it, is therefore spectral, like light. More importantly, as in the case of light, the rainbow is only visible if all the colors are represented. Likewise, power is most effective, when all the tools along the power spectrum, ranging from hard to soft are represented whether by a single country or a group of countries forming alliances.

The consideration of power as one entity consisting of different types of tools will make it easier to assemble a "tool-kit" in the future, better reflecting the complexity of each situation. It will also enable us to make better choices for the way we use our ever-decreasing resources and make a dynamic approach possible instead of the traditional static one. A holistic approach will force institutions to work closer resulting in a more effective impact.

This spectral conceptualization will result in a rethinking of the hierarchy of power, which is especially important today. While arguably, to have global influence a country or a group of countries must be able to wield the whole spectrum of power (strategic-military, tactical-military, economic, diplomatic and human-social-cultural), the importance of providers of the parts cannot be underestimated.

At this point, Nye's Smart Power concept must be mentioned as it differs from our conceptualization of spectral power. Our main argument in this chapter is that countries would benefit more from understanding the different aspects of power in international relations as factors supporting and complementing each other instead of separating them into two groups. Nye's Smart Power relies on the dual understanding of power utilizing what is needed of each in the required amounts. But our linear conceptualization allows scholars and policy makers to view all aspects of power without isolation or exclusion.

It could, if reason prevails, result in a pooling of resources by smaller countries. One good example already under way is the way Nordic countries (Sweden, Finland, Denmark, Norway and Iceland) are working to align their militaries as well as their cultural, societal and diplomatic influences.

The underlying interest in developing the concept of *spectral power* is economic. A better understanding of the entirety and complexity of the tools in our toolbox; a better and more conceptual framing of the relationship between the individual elements—the way they interact and the way they exert their influence—and a better grasp of the cultural and geographical limitations to their use, and the timeframes within which they can be used, will result in better economics of power. It will lead to a wiser use of resources, a better institutional distribution of tasks within and among like-minded countries, and a much more effective and even distribution of burdens among countries sharing the same values.

Popular Culture:
The Hard Soft Power Tool that Helped Win the Cold War

The importance of the West's non-military influence on the East during the Cold War cannot be overstated. It came early, and it came in many forms. It had a thorough effect on generation after generation, and one can state confidently that its impact contributed enormously and early to the weakening, and eventually demise of communism.

The West administered its non-military power tools wisely and with sophistication. Governments spent enormous amounts on what the East called "Western propaganda" but it was more than that, much more. The constant "bombardment" by Radio Free Europe, the Voice of America or the BBC of the public of Eastern Europe including the then Soviet Union, had a huge impact. Its success was also due to the scarcity of information in communist countries and the heavy-handed censorship and lack of transparency resulting from the dictatorial nature of the political system there. Western broadcasts were a huge contrast. It was also made possible by the advances in radio broadcasting technology. It was Soft Power at its best. Still broadcasting in itself would not have made all the difference. Technology, without the right content, is just that: technology, a static tool.

Western influence was not just a result of smart and well-organized communication, although it is true that taxpayers' money was well spent on such efforts as youth and cultural exchanges, cultural centers and American libraries attached to U.S. Embassies. The credibility of the broadcasts, Western literature and cultural centers was founded in more desirable lifestyles, a higher standard of living, and a superior quality as well as abundance of consumer goods and services. There was a strong understanding among the public of the communist countries that all this was possible because of a pluralistic and competitive democratic system, and the market economy. If VOA and Radio Free Europe were the hardware, the popular culture in the form of rock music, Hollywood, fashion and literature was the software. The incredible power of popular culture broke all boundaries and became a formidable element in the "ideological warfare," providing striking contrast to Soviet propaganda, which was caught lying day in and day out. The West influenced the East by persuasion and attraction. Popular culture was the "thing" that the youths of the East could associate with easily. It was their connection to the West. It was their "internet," even if it was one-way communication.

Rock music stood out among the "tools." The medium was easily embraced with its appealing rhythms and melodies. The Beatles, the Stones, the Hollies and the Kinks, David Bowie, Steve Winwood, Eric Clapton, Elvis Presley, Carol King, Jimi Hendrix, Neil Young, Bob Dylan, Frank Zappa, the Velvet Underground, Donovan, Janis Joplin and all their friends and colleagues looked happy and colorful. They were great musicians playing great music. Their music was a statement on freedom of thought and expression. By embracing and emulating this, those generations of people in the East acquired a formidable tool of empowerment.

The more the communist governments tried to keep rock music out, the more it was coveted and embraced. When young people listened to their radios under their bed covers, in the privacy of their rooms or in the company of other youths, the frontiers disappeared; they became one with their peers in the West. This act in itself made them, in their minds, Western. This was an enemy communist authorities had a hard time fighting. They tried and they lost.

Other attributes of the Western lifestyle had perhaps less deep but still important and symbolic effects. Everyday items such as blue jeans became a symbol of the Western-minded. Wearing Levi's was a statement of who you were, of your political and ideological preferences. Levi's was a coveted fashion item, and for many constituted a way of expressing disapproval of the drabness of "socialist" society. Rock-and-roll music and Levi's jeans were a different expression of the same: the West's Soft Power. Industrial products lived a life of their own. Coca Cola was considered a magic drug. Having experienced it was a sign of exclusivity for a long time. All this had an incredible fermenting effect on societies in the East. During the Cold War, the West's Soft Power was at its absolute best. Then, when rock music, Levi's or for that matter Coca Cola became easily accessible, they lost their edge.

What are the lessons learned? One should *not* think that popular culture or any of its elements are a remedy for all societies at all times, or that we can mindlessly "deploy" it to any part of the world. That would be simplistic. But we should not underestimate the attraction of rock music and popular culture for the youths of countries like Iran, Azerbaijan or even North Korea. One should rather think of rock music as a metaphor: each generation, each culture needs to find its own "rock music".

The Spectral Power Toolbox

The Color Red

The importance of visible and reliable "Hard-hard" Power can be neither underestimated nor disregarded. The strength and presence of credible and visible "Hard-hard" Power is the underlying and fundamental basis upon which other aspects of global or regional power can be built and without which Soft Power tools are essentially ineffective in the strategic power game. No doubt this century will be about the realignment of the tools and means of power delivery reflecting the decreasing likelihood of strategic conflict between nuclear-armed nations and the global battlefield. However, the possession of strategic military means will still be a defining element in the global influence of powers. Strategic forces, global reach, strategic lift capabilities and simultaneous war-fighting capabilities will continue to be role defining. In the case of Europe and the United States, NATO should become not less but more important, as alliances will gain more and not less prominence. While in this chapter we do not discuss the future of NATO in its complexity, it is important to state that rethinking its possible and advanced partnerships within and beyond Europe will be necessary. Only if Europe will take on more military responsibility in its back yard and globally, will it become a global force. Indeed, Europe and the United States are learning once again that without the military and internal security assets to counter extreme ideology, both radical Islam and a resurgent Russia, will continue to threaten the Western way of life. Its economic power, however important, will not be sufficient.

The Colors Orange and Green

Hard-soft and Soft-hard Power tools, including non-warlike military interventions, are a means to influence a given strategic, political, social and economic environment, and in some cases challenge political authority and institutions. These are instruments of change and influence, which can alter situations, perceptions and attitudes for the long term. These are "weapons" which often require major efforts from opponents to counter. In many cases these instruments involve major commitments and investment from governments and civil society. They can be attached to or combined with military efforts, at times "military" in appearance. They are deployed consciously and their presence or absence can be strategic and have long-term impacts. These tools can constitute a relatively short-term action with lasting effects, or they can spell a long-term commitment to a given context.

The absence of "Hard-soft" Power in certain instances can have devastating effects as was the case in the Iraq War: economic and currency chaos ensued, as a result of which basic utility services diminished, and museums that once held the patrimony of Western civilization were looted. The protection of cultural heritage sites during or after military conflict is a good example of a hard-soft power tool. Protecting cultural sites demonstrates respect as it addresses identity and dignity of a people, and has a lasting and comforting effect.

Elements of strategic "Soft-hard" or "Hard-soft" tools of power can be an economic necessity as well. Increasingly, there is a debate about the effectiveness, and the long-term impact of aid-policies of rich countries. There are serious doubts about their ability to generate overall improvement in the lives of the citizens of aided countries. The unfortunate conclusion in many cases is that aid has led to the cementing of elites, who have enriched themselves by appropriating some of the enormous amounts of money flowing through their hands, to the detriment of their societies. The altruistic aid approach has in most cases not yielded long-term influence. While this was clearly not part of the consideration, it seems more and more evident that it should be.

It turns out that elements of "Hard-soft" Power, like U.S. efforts to help curb the AIDS epidemic in Africa ("the Bush Institute's Global Health Initiative")—a government effort, or the attempt to help eradicate malaria ("The Bill Gates Foundation")—a private initiative, had a lot more impact in promoting Western values and long-term interests, which are not just economic and strategic.

We discussed the enormous strategic influence of popular culture and rock music in the previous section. It is important to understand that it was indeed strategic. The mechanism through which it had its strategic and indeed political impact is still un-researched. Nevertheless it definitely belongs to the "Hard-soft" category.

The Color Blue

Soft-soft power is more subtle in its appearance. It is in some cases not even the result of conscious planning and deployment, and while it can be "deployed" by governments, in many cases it is better off on its own or done best by non-governmental organizations (NGOs), though many of them are not perceived as independent or wholly altruistic.[2] Soft-soft power is deployed to assist and solve major social problems, modify perceptions, be a source of change based on Western values, represent the better angles of our societies and alter the lives of individuals by providing them with new opportunities.

Cultural diplomacy finds a home in this category. Good examples are cultural institutions such as the Cervantes Institute, Alliance française, Goethe Institute or the Peace Corps. The closing of U.S. libraries and cultural centers in Eastern Europe or in the Middle East since 9/11 or even in India (the American Center in Hyderabad, India, once housed the largest library of American books outside the United States but now has fallen into neglect and disrepair) has deprived the United States of an important, effective and also relatively cheap strategic means of influence in those countries.[3]

---

[2]As an example, see Ronelle Burger's and Trudy Owens' research paper (2008), "Promoting Transparency in the NGO Sector: Examining the Availability and Reliability of Self Reported Data," Centre for Research in Economic Development and International Trade, University of Nottingham.

[3]See Cynthia P. Schneider and Kristina Nelson (2008). *Mightier than the Sword: Arts and Culture in the U.S.-Muslim World Relationship*. The Sabban Center for Midddle East at Brookings. p. 37 http://www.brookings.edu/~/media/research/files/papers/2008/6/islamic% 20world%20schneider/06_islamic_world_schneider.pdf (last accessed: June1st, 2014).

Private sector organizations can also make a difference, adding to a country's "Soft-soft" power via the promotion of transparency and the teaching of best practices in host countries. Some of these private sector efforts have been a key component in the development of certain new democracies. In the case of IBM or GE, for example, the corporate values and practices for entering tenders, managing and compensating employees, offering benefits, and promoting tolerance have infused the societies and the marketplace in nascent democracies with higher expectations of corporate behavior—often reinforced by the diplomatic mission to those countries.

The Brackish Part of the Spectrum

Some power actions, however, fall into a special category—what we would call the "brackish" part of the power spectrum, a certain grey zone between hard and soft. Their "hardness" depends on where and when and under what circumstances the means are deployed. The visit of the New York Symphony to North Korea certainly falls into the category of "Hard-soft" power, defined not by the means of delivery, but by the context and environment within which it is deployed. Officially sanctioned and diplomatically negotiated, the Symphony went on a targeted cultural exchange visit to expose North Koreans to both the cultured and civilized aspects of an America branded as otherwise war-mongering by the Pyongyang leadership. It must have had a huge impact on the elite of North Korea. While important, the New York Symphony's visit would certainly not have the same impact in today's Prague or Paris.

Mention must be made of public policy as a tool. Equating public policy with Soft Power, as is often done and wrongly so, is denying the complexity of Soft Power. Public policy is a government effort to explain the actions of a given country in pursuit of its interests and promotion of its values. Soft Power, however, is a complex set of instruments including everything from the economy and business, culture and education, the interaction between societies and individual relationships, to a set of other instruments. Soft Power is not only a set of tools, it is also a *mindset*. The latter will employ public policy whenever it is needed. Public policy is an inevitable aspect of Soft Power, and its importance cannot be ignored, nor should it be exaggerated as a magic weapon. It is a challenging tool, because it can easily backfire if its target audience dismisses it as mere propaganda.

Public policy, however, is truly important. It must employ the new means of communication. Yet, there must be clarity about the limitations of technology. The possibilities are vast but should not be overemphasized. The internet, Facebook and Twitter are just technological platforms. They can be turned into instruments only with the right approach and perhaps "the individual touch." Otherwise, they will be dismissed as mere marketing tools, instead of being a mainstay of Soft Power. In the end, whatever the technology, it is the content that matters. Facebook and Twitter will soon be overtaken by something new, but the imperative to use our Soft Power will remain.

Measuring the Entire Spectrum of Power

Measuring Hard Power is not a problem while Soft Power, as part of the power toolbox, has been an understudied subfield in international relations. No wonder policymakers, for better or worse, rely to a great extent on intuition, while power should not rely on intuition only, but on the ability to measure. In order for the complex power toolbox to be optimized, new methods of measuring power must be developed. Other reasons include the rapid change of technology and the changing nature of communication. All the colors and their shades, not just the color red, should be properly measured, as objectively as possible. We can already see problems arising from the inability to do so. Our investment in the revolutions of North Africa is an example. To have a measurement method that is capable of identifying and capturing the entire power spectrum, scholars will have to focus on power capabilities first. Conceptualizing the entire spectrum of power and not stopping at only two colors of the spectrum will allow policy makers and political scientists to study the cultural, historical and social strengths of societies, and utilize the most intriguing and attractive elements of countries' customs.

Hard Power has served as a foundation of power literature to which most scholars try to compare or contrast their Soft Power measurement. The Correlates of War is just one of the great examples of creating and measuring military indicators globally. Since the beginning of the 21st century, there has been an increasing number of attempts to measure the Soft Power end of the power spectrum, with little or limited success. The measurement of Soft Power and the other shades of the power spectrum are clearly a challenge for scholars and policy makers.

Joseph Nye has referred to public opinion data to indicate the success or failure of a country's Soft Power. More particularly, Nye has used the Pew Research Global Attitude Project surveys to capture foreign populations' attitude towards the United States in 2002.[4] Nye also approaches the measurement of Soft Power as a combination of perceived attitude and money spent on public diplomacy.[5] Yet he only measures the resources spent in one year (money spent on public diplomacy and on Hard Power) and focuses on the survey results of foreign countries' attitudes and attitude changes towards the United States. Similar measurements of the parallel changes in resources would be a great addition to the measurement.

Gregory G. Holyk builds on Nye's survey-based approach; Holyk uses the Chicago Council on Global Affairs survey to further study and develop a method of measuring and comparing Soft Power among countries[6]. His study represents a great example of the difficulties facing scholars trying to capture the impact of Soft Power. Its design is based on one-time survey data, so it does not capture changes in public opinion. Its reliance on the general public versus the elite may result in a less-informed response about the selected country's perception of Soft Power.

These are just some of the aspects of the problem of measuring the non-hard aspects of power, which calls for intensified multidisciplinary efforts.

---

[4] See the Pew Research Global Attitudes Project 2002 Report: http://www.pewglobal.org/files/2002/12/2002-Report-Final-Updated.pdf (last accessed: June 1st, 2014).

[5] While Joseph Nye (2004) divides the power spectrum into hard and soft parts, his results only demonstrate the selected countries' resource commitment level in each type of power and do not include other programs or institutions that serve other shades of power. He initiates a significant and eye opening conversation on U.S. lack of Soft Power budgetary commitments compared to other countries, especially considering their total budget.

[6] While Holyk (2011) includes multiple dimensions to measure Soft Power, some of which we conceptualize as Soft-hard and Soft-soft powers, including economic, human capital, diplomatic, cultural and political, he solely relies on survey results of six countries' split sampling answers combined into a standardized score to arrive at the combined rating of each country's Soft Power perception. Holyk's indices are weighted equally in the final score despite the various numbers of questions in the five dimensions included in the survey. Finally, to better capture perceived influence versus actual influence of Soft Power, Holyk applies "a bivariate regression on all questions' scores."

The United States and Europe:
Mars and Venus? Of Course Not!

It has been argued in the political and intellectual circles of Europe that Europe's real possibilities lie in the wielding of its Soft Power. On the one hand, this argument assumes that Europe will not experience major threats in the future. On the other hand, it is held that these could be averted by the political-diplomatic influence Europe wields as an economic super power. The argument assumes that Europe is not part of the global strategic power game—of the global security equation. It also assumes that strategic military threats are of the past, and that a strategic confrontation is inconceivable. There is reason to suspect that there is also an expectation, that if push came to shove, NATO [meaning the United States] would make good on its Article 5 obligations regarding mutual defense, so Europe need not to worry much about its own defense. This position suggests that Europe does not have global ambitions, or if it does, it falsely assumes that its Soft Power will serve all its power needs. Europe, of course, is not demilitarized. But without global ambitions, the willingness to invest in, and more importantly the willingness to use its military assets—its Hard Power, and thus its global influence—are waning.

The United States, no doubt, would make good on its obligations, in particular enshrined in the North Atlantic Treaty and its Article 5, in its own interest. This European assumption, however, ignores the tectonic changes in the American society and the depth of public fatigue after two ineffective and inconclusive wars in Iraq and Afghanistan. The United States has also rebalanced toward Asia, suggesting the relativization of Europe (although Europeans have exaggerated and misunderstood the motives). The United States will continue striving to possess the most advanced and dominant military force in the world, but Europe cannot expect U.S. commitments in regions that are Europe's backyard to continue forever.

The United States expects greater burden sharing by Europeans. It expects Europeans to rethink their military contributions within the NATO Alliance and within the European Union. Perhaps that will only happen out of necessity, but it must happen. It ties in with the need for Europe to rethink its global ambitions. If it thinks about itself as a global player, it will have to do a number of things. It will have to take ownership of its own security, and beyond. The United States could slowly but steadily withdraw from the Middle East not the least, because of its declining interest in the region, as its strategic interests change in light of the energy revolution in the United States and the broader Atlantic Basin. Due to the increasing reliance on its own energy production as a result of the shale revolution, as well as the increasing role of Africa and South America as providers of energy, the United States will rethink its commitments in the Middle East. The threats and challenges emanating from North Africa and the Middle East will increasingly become Europe's problems.

Terrorism and impending refugee crises, requiring serious military commitments, will continue to be a challenge, which Europe will have to deal with as well, probably on its own. There is a growing under-standing that terrorism will have to be fought with multiple means, including ever-more sophisticated military means and tools, at the source, that respond to the fast-growing technological sophistication. Recent crises, like Libya and Mali, show that the European Union is not ready politically, militarily or institutionally to take on these threats effectively on its own.

All this calls for Europe to embrace the concept of spectral-power, and to reinforce and rethink its Hard Power capabilities. Presently it does not have the capability to do all of the above, in addition to its lack of political will. It should stop spending the peace dividends, which have been in deficit for some time, and realize that there is nothing more to spend. European elites need to go through the painful intellectual and political exercise of establishing foundations to reinforce the power toolbox, first and foremost elements of Hard Power. As a result, Europe will be a better partner for the United States, and it will also be able to promote better its own interests in the world. The United States is rethinking its power toolbox. Europe must do the same.

Conclusion

Europe is not simply the beautiful Venus, and the United States is definitely not only Mars. The United States has formidable Hard Power, but it also has equally formidable reserves of Soft Power resources. Europe can and should wield its Soft Power based on its traditional economic might and vast culture. Global strategic influence, however, cannot be achieved by Soft Power alone. The attraction of the United States is under threat and could decline further. A better coordination and smarter cooperation is needed across the Atlantic to maximize the impact of power instruments, the spectral power toolbox, at the disposal of both. There are and will be situations when Europe can wield Soft Power better and more effectively than the United States, and when small countries can do so better than big ones. This should not turn, however, into a beauty contest. The transatlantic community must invest heavily in the instruments of both Soft and Hard Power. In this non-zero sum game, there is a need for more Soft Power, not less Hard Power, and perhaps even more of the in-between tools for the sake of becoming more effective, more attractive and more economic. The different forms of power are not formulaically counterbalancing. They are mutually dependent and mutually reinforcing.

Both sides of the Atlantic have been taking each other for granted. Europe and the United States have considered their relationship rock solid, as strong in peace as it was in war, hot or cold. This is wrong, as no relationship can be taken for granted forever, unless it is nurtured and is given continued support from its citizenry. Even though the transatlantic community is considered a family—or maybe because it sees itself as a family—members need constant reassurance and nurturing of their relationship.

The foundation of the Western belief in its power resources, hard or soft, lies in its belief in human rights and freedom. It is the belief that allows the West to reconcile its interests with the needs and interests of the international community. This is not blind faith in Western values. Integrity does not mean rigidity. It means that the West and its institutions are able and willing to take into account the interests of others while not losing sight of its own people and the values for which it stands.

All this calls for a *spectral power* mindset.

References

Burger, Ronelle, and Owens, Trudy, Research Paper (2008), *Promoting transparency in the NGO sector: Examining the availability and reliability of self reported data*, Centre for Research in Economic Development and International Trade, University of Nottingham.

Holyk, Gregory, G. 2011. Paper Tiger? Chinese Soft Power in East Asia. *Political Science Quarterly*. Volume 126, Issue 2, pages 223–254, Summer.

Kounalakis, Markos and Simonyi, Andras. 2011. *The Hard Truth About Soft Power*. Figueroa Press, USC Bookstore.

McClory, Jonathan. 2013. *The New Persuaders III. A 2012 Global Ranking of Soft Power*. Institute for Government.

Nye, Joseph Jr. 2004. *Soft Power: The Means to Success in World Politics*. Public Affairs. New York.

Nye, Joseph Jr. 2011. *The Future of Power*. Public Affairs. New York.

(The) Pew Research Center For The People & The Press, 2002. *What People think in 2002*, Final Report.

Schneider, Cynthia P., and Nelson, Kristina (2008). *Mightier than the Sword: Arts and Culture in the U.S.-Muslim World Relationship*. The Saban Center for Midddle East at Brookings. Washington DC.

Chapter 3

To Collude or Collide?
How Combining Hard Power and Soft Power
Can Be a Problem or the Solution

Stacia George

Power is a term that is taken for granted. We talk about it all the time but have differing views of what the term represents. What, exactly, is power, and why is it so desired? At its most fundamental, power is the ability to influence, or if necessary, force an individual, institution, or state to behave in a way that is in your interest or at a minimum, does not work against your interest.

All actors—individuals, groups, governments—must understand how to effectively wield power in order to attain their goals. Parents, gangs, governments, and social movements can all quickly fail when they misunderstand power.

For the basis of this discussion, I divide the tools that individuals, groups, and governments use to achieve power into two categories: Hard Power (defined for these purposes as kinetic power equating physical and/or military might) and Soft Power (defined as non-kinetic methods of power including measures that bring economic, political, and social influence). Both types of power are desirable and useful, depending on whom one is trying to influence and what would influence them. When used effectively together, they are referred to as "Smart Power," and even terrorist organizations have begun to recognize the value of this comprehensive toolbox through both military measures and development and political campaigns. For example, Hezbollah has long employed a dual strategy of Hard Power through terrorist attack actions and Soft Power through rapid and large social support programs like food, education, and shelter provision for citizens living in areas where Hezbollah operates. Gangs frequently enforce their territorial control through brute force against anyone who does not obey them, but at the same time will try to obtain and maintain community support through activities such as sponsoring community events and/or providing material support for schools.

While the existence of Hard and Soft Power together may be a recipe for supposed Smart Power it may not be the formula for smart policy. A greater quantity of resident power does not always translate into more effective power, and combining Soft and Hard Power approaches do not always result in net gains. At times, the application of either one or the other could lead to greater success than using a combined approach. This is the paradox of "Smart Power": simply mixing Soft and Hard Power without a well-designed strategy could, in the end, lead to less power rather than more. This is why good policy making can be compromised when Soft, Hard and Smart Power are introduced; the assumption that Hard and Soft Power combined equate to *smarter power* and therefore to smarter policy can lead decision makers to adopt policies that they think will be better, but in practice are less effective.

In order to ensure that the smartest policies are adopted, one must first understand the conditions under which combining U.S. Hard and Soft Power approaches can result in a whole that is smaller or greater than its parts. Using both Hard and Soft Power together requires careful coordination of strategy and tactics that if not managed well can diminish the effectiveness of Hard and Soft Power elements. This phenomenon has been seen in Vietnam, Iraq and Afghanistan where large sums of kinetic military and Soft Power resources, such as military capacity building, and economic and development aid, did not appear to create proportionally larger results. In short, increased level of inputs does not necessarily equate to proportional increases in outcomes. It has been enormously challenging to get the U.S. military to accept this formula as their own Hard Power calculus has long held that a large quantity of resources and an "all hands on deck" approach to a problem set will always bring a faster solution. But what determines outcomes when using Smart Power is not just the inputs but also the degree to which the approaches consider the fundamentals of power. In order to have power, one must have three components: an understanding of what behavior change is sought, a common and accurate understanding of what will encourage behavior change in a target audience, and the leverage to create that shift. Even with these components, additional challenges can arise when mixing Hard and Soft Power.

Components of Effective Power

Possessing the tools of power is not the same as successfully wielding power. For example, the United States has large quantities of financial and military resources at its disposal. But there are still instances where it may not be as powerful and able to influence on the ground regardless of how much money it spends (e.g. some parts of Afghanistan and Africa) nor how many threats they make of using military force (e.g., Syria, Iran). Smart power is about the ability to harness different types of power to influence the right behaviors, not just wave different tools of power around to demonstrate that they exist. Unfortunately, sometimes U.S. policy becomes more about putting as many tools of power on the table ("all hands on deck," "whole of government") rather than determining which and how these tools will translate into actual power.

In order to take the tools of power and turn them into actual power, three key components must exist:

1. *A clear understanding of what behavior change is sought through the use of that power:* A hammer would not be an appropriate instrument if one's objective was to smooth a piece of wood. But that hammer would be perfect if you were trying to nail two pieces of wood together. The same applies to the decision-making process used to determine what type(s) of power to use. Organizations can fall prey to Maslow's Maxim—when the only tool available is a hammer, then every problem begins to look like a nail. In the U.S. foreign policy-making process, determining which behavior you are trying to influence can be easily lost in the shuffle of multiple priorities, actions, and players. Conversations can be clouded by people looking at all of the resources across the board and how to mobilize them rather than starting with the question: "What are we trying to achieve?" Additionally, bureaucracy can decimate big-picture thinking and place process at the forefront at the expense of deliberate planning and action. The result—U.S. actors often forget why they were using those tools of power in the first place. When I asked U.S. military personnel deploying to Afghanistan to tell me the U.S. objective in Afghanistan, instead of the objective, I received responses that focused on tactics (kill militants, disrupt transit routes), methods (civil affairs projects, cash for work, community patrolling), and interim results (improve Afghan

army capacity, make sure the government is less corrupt, stop poppy cultivation, improve roads). Tools of power are used differently depending on the objective sought. For example, a road project with an objective of improving transportation only might be implemented by a Civil Affairs team in order to complete it quickly while it would be run and implemented with the Afghan Government if the objective of the road project were to serve as a tool for helping the Afghan government to learn how to design and execute civil works projects. It depends on whether improved transportation or government capacity would be more influential on key actors' behaviors in order to achieve larger strategic objectives. But before one can determine what action would encourage the desired behavior, one must first understand what change in behavior they are seeking through the use of their power.

2. All actors must have a common and accurate understanding of what will encourage the desired behavior in the target audience: To achieve the effective application of power, one must first have a common and accurate understanding of what behaviors the United States is trying to encourage and what will encourage the target actor to adopt those behaviors. Achieving a correct understanding of how to influence the target actors' behavior is no small feat. This requires an accurate understanding of the target audience including what motivates and drives their decision-making process. Actors, however, must first let go of their preconceptions, frequently drawn from one's own perspective. As any married couple will tell you, even if you know and have lived with someone for years, it does not mean that it is obvious how to influence the other person's behavior.

These assumptions can become a greater roadblock when working with actors in foreign contexts. Understanding what makes another actor tick within your own cultural context is hard enough, but it is even more challenging if you first have to understand the context from which the actor come and within which the actors operates. Even if you come from a so-called similar culture, there may still be disparities. For example, northerners and southerners within the U.S. will tell you that there are aspects of each other's cultures that they do not understand. A similar circumstance exists with people who are from urban versus rural areas.

Attempts have been made to overcome these obstacles. Entire "human terrain teams" have been dedicated in Afghanistan to help coalition forces to understand their counterparts and determine the appropriate method for influencing behaviors of key actors and institutions in Afghanistan. But these efforts can only narrow the void, not eliminate it. In Pakistan's Federally Administered Tribal Areas, despite in-depth analysis by outsiders, the general assumption for a long time among international actors and even Pakistani non-governmental organizations was that the local population supported the militants and their views. The resulting assumption was that eliminating the militants included targeting the local population. But most locals did not support the militants' viewpoints. Instead, the main reason why militants were able to flourish was because the local population was unable to defend themselves against the militants and had to concede the territory to them. In fact, the local population generally did not agree with the militants. If the intervention had been designed based on the initial assumption that all locals were militants or militant supporters, they would have lost the opportunity to use the local population to help eliminate the militants. Instead, targeting the local population would have increased support for the militants rather than reduce it.

In addition to an accurate understanding of how to achieve influence, all actors within an environment must have the same understanding of what the behavior is that they are trying to create. This is especially important for an institution trying to exert power. If one part of that institution has one understanding correct, but others have a different understanding, then the efforts of those who do understand correctly are still hamstrung because the others might be working at cross purposes with them or their efforts cannot be leveraged. This is the reason why it is so important to have inter-agency coordination and/or to diminish the amount of actors trying to exert power on an actor or environment. The same dynamic occurs in the international arena where success requires the international community to be working off the same page. This is very challenging when there are competing political agendas driving both Soft and Hard Power approaches.

3. Leverage: The good cop/bad cop scenario has withstood the test of time for a reason. It provides a perfect illustration of how Soft and Hard Power could work together effectively. The good cop uses a charming personality and incentives or "carrots" to encourage the culprit to give in. The bad cop threatens the culprit with harsh punishment, or, "sticks" if he is not cooperative. Both roles are important. Each one has an element of power to influence the culprit's behavior. Together, the two players can have significant power over the culprit. Why? Because they are working towards a common objective of targeting the person responsible for the crime and using a broader range of pressure points to influence the subject. But what happens when they do not work together or have a common purpose? What if the good cop offers incentives for the criminal to confess but the bad cop does not offer the threat of jail or a fine? The culprit does not have an incentive to cooperate. Or what if the good cop is not able to offer an incentive? The culprit might choose to not cooperate and take their chances with the justice system instead. The result could be costly court proceedings and a possibility that the culprit is not convicted which is in neither the good nor the bad cop's interest.

This case illustrates how Hard and Soft Power can individually be influential but are much more powerful if they can be synchronized towards the same objective. We see this same scenario play out at an international and state level. For example, the Mano Dura programs in El Salvador and other parts of Central America in the 1980s and 1990s focused on hard targeting and imprisoning any youth who might appear to be a gang member. While a large number of youths ended up in prison, this did not address the problem because many youths who were not gang members were quickly recruited into gangs while in the prisons or turned against the authorities as a result of their unfair imprisonment. If Soft Power elements such as employment, education, or youth programs had been more deliberately offered to gang members who wanted to leave, the Hard Power efforts would have had more leverage in decreasing the number of gang members.

Soft Power methods can be misperceived as being too focused on concession. Diplomats and development workers are frequently perceived as soft tree huggers who give too much without respecting the reality of Hard Power. But make no mistake. Simply equating Hard Power with sticks and Soft Power with carrots is misleading.

Soft Power elements can be and are frequently wielded as sticks, and this is the case when those Soft Power tools have leverage over other actors. With leverage, their use or their removal can have serious consequences for individuals and nations. Threats of rescinding trade deals, development programs, and bailout funding are extremely effective as are threats to withdraw U.S. support for IMF and World Bank funding or support in the UN Security Council or other political forums. A negative rating in addressing human trafficking in the annual U.S. Trafficking in Persons report can result in a country losing its development assistance.

The United States pulled out its development funding for Pakistan in protest over its nuclear program and ended development support for Colombia in the early 1990s to encourage the Colombian Government to change some of its heavy-handed tactics and extreme corruption. Money talks, and once the Colombian Government did come around to a new approach to address the FARC and corruption issues that was acceptable to the U.S., money went back on the table as encouragement. That was Plan Colombia. Soft Power tools are frequently used as carrots, but when actors are in need of political, economic or social support, the threat of removing these incentives can be extremely effective if there is sufficient leverage.

In order to achieve sufficient leverage, three requirements must be met: *the ability to remove, change, apply or offer carrots and sticks; consistency; and credibility.*

1. The ability to remove, change, apply or offer carrots and sticks. When the good cop cannot offer a deal and/or does not have the ability to take the deal off of the table, then she loses leverage. There must be flexibility in how the Soft Power incentives are tailored and applied. Likewise, if the bad cop cannot wield her stick of penalties such as fines or jail time, she is powerless. This may seem obvious, but in reality, offering and taking away carrots and sticks is a lot harder than we may think. In Afghanistan, for example, the United States gains some leverage by being able to offer development, economic, political, and security support as incentives, but the United States is limited in its ability to take away those incentives because of the high level of investment and commitment made, and the difficulty in withdrawing those resources both logistically and politically. In this case, and similar cases where the United States is highly invested, the United States has more limited credibility when it suggests it may pull development aid. Syria provides another example. Throughout 2011 and into early

2012, the U.S. ability to apply sticks against the Assad regime was limited by blocked UN Security Council resolutions and a domestic wariness towards deploying troops towards another overseas conflict. This inability to apply sticks resulted in the United States having limited power over the Syrian government.

2. Credibility. To achieve credibility, the threat or offer must be timely and consistent. Quickly living up to one's end of a bargain sets the stage for credibility of future applications of power. This is why rapid action and results after a peace negotiation are so important. Each party must quickly demonstrate that they are credible. Otherwise, the loss of credibility in one area will quickly translate into loss of credibility in others. This was the FARC's mistake in Colombia. The Colombian Government began negotiations with the FARC in good faith, but the FARC continued offensive operations and reneged on agreements in the negotiations to the point where the Colombian Government took negotiations off the table and resumed offensive operations. Credibility is also challenging to achieve when the application of power is dependent upon multiple actors to be coordinated and in agreement, because the greater the tools and actors, the harder it is to respond quickly. Slow response time can diminish credibility by making it look like the actor is not acting in good faith or that they will be unable to deliver on future promises.

3. Consistency. Actors have the greatest influence when they maintain consistent positions. This can be hard to achieve. It is hard enough for one actor or institution to be consistent in its actions. To be consistent with other actors is even more challenging. Actors frequently have their own agendas without strategic links to those of others. In political matters, one can have actors with the same agenda but who do not bother to discuss, nevertheless coordinate, with others. This disconnect can frequently be attributed to time constraints in regards to coordination—some organizations simply do not have the staff and time to coordinate. Other organizations feel that they can do it better alone—but often this is simply because they are focusing on streamlining bureaucratic processes and neglecting the need for a consistent interagency or international response. The U.S. Government struggles with this particular problem not just with regards to interagency coordination, but even with internal coordination within individual organizations.

Although it may be too much to hope for all international actors in a country of intervention to maintain a similar position, at a minimum, U.S. actors must strive to maintain consistent positions. Arguably, this is the raison d'être of the National Security Council and the plethora of interagency working groups attended by Assistant, Deputy Assistant and Under Secretaries on a daily basis in Washington. Indeed, if everyone agreed to the same principles of how they want tools of power to be used, their power would increase exponentially.

Consistency can be a real challenge in some areas such as human rights and democracy because they can be trumped by higher priority objectives. For example, the U.S. Government was able to push the agenda of the responsibility to protect individuals from atrocities in the case of Libya, but has been unable to be responsive to this agenda in Syria in a significant way because other political and security objectives override it. This means that the United States can look less credible in its democracy agenda. Regardless, actors must strive to be consistent because consistency gives credibility to their negotiations and actions. Consistency also gives leverage by ensuring that there are no openings for avoiding the application of the tools of power. Consistency also makes it easier for actors to read others' intentions.

Achieving leverage is significantly harder when there are multiple actors in an environment. The ability to remove and offer incentives must be consistently applied by all actors trying to have influence, and consistency is easily compromised with multiple actors wielding various carrots and sticks. For example, if an actor decides to use development projects (a component of Soft Power) to promote women's rights, these might require women's participation in the decision-making process as one of the criteria for receiving a project. If this principles is adhered to and projects are in no circumstances provided without this requirement in place, then either groups will come around and start including women or they will forego the benefits of aid programs. The level at which they will change their behavior to receive the project is determined by how much that project reflects what they think is important. If beneficiaries decide not to include women, then a project is not provided and precious resources are not wasted on something that would not support the promotion of women's rights.

What if another U.S. government actor comes along without the same agenda in mind? They could decide to implement projects regardless of whether women are involved because supporting women's rights might not be their organizational objective. The original development projects lose their power to encourage men to support women's rights. This creates a gap and could result in a failure to attain overarching policy objectives. The Chinese Government's approach to development projects across the world has similar effects by sometimes diminishing the power and influence of other countries' development projects simply because they offer much and require little in exchange, except for access to markets and infrastructure.

This challenge of consistency can also explain trends such as why corruption has been so hard to stop in Afghanistan. Even if one actor decides that they will not use a particular vendor or work with a particular government official until they change their corrupt ways, they will have no power over that vendor or official unless everybody else in the international arena agrees that they too will walk away from that vendor and government official. The capability to exert power over the corrupt individual is nullified by the presence of others who do not have the same priority. Similarly, individual travel sanctions are less powerful when only one or two countries put them in place rather than a coalition of key countries such as the European Union and the United States together because individuals do not feel that much of an impact on their lives.

Power and influence are similarly affected by the comparative magnitude of actors' Soft and Hard Power when competing for influence. Even with the right Hard and Soft Power approaches in place in terms of type, trying to wield Soft or Hard Power in places when the power and influence of other actors is much larger, can be challenging. In Nepal, the United States has some power simply by being a global leader and for some Soft Power assets that it offers, but its power can be easily trumped by China or India whose Soft Power assets (geopolitical relevance and the amount of resources that they provide) are more influential in Nepal. In other cases, the sheer scale of Hard or Soft Power can be a factor. In key strategic or mineral rich countries, China frequently offers comparatively enormous financial contributions and development projects as part of its Soft Power, and frequently has more influence there as a result.

In some countries, small quantities or costless offers of political support can have enormous influence, but it depends on the target actor's calculus of what is important to them. Being able to offer something of value to the other actor will influence their behavior. It can be as basic as support for a vote in the UN General Assembly that might not be difficult for the United States to provide but is crucial to the other actor. Or it can be providing something tangible that the actor needs. Arguably, in the Congo from 2003 to 2006, the United States was able to influence affairs to a point because of its political weight in the international community, and due to its large contributions to the peace process and development in the country. At the same time, however, this was relative because the USAID Mission budget could only exert some influence given the high level of need, and the Congolese government knew that they would not have to contend with U.S. Hard Power.

It is important to reiterate that quantity is not usually a determining factor for how powerful an element of power can be when considering "Smart Power" approaches. Larger quantities of Soft and Hard Power can, at times, equate to greater influence but only if they are the right types of Soft and Hard Power, and if they take into account the dynamics of influence on the local actor. Sometimes, it does not take much in order to sway behaviors one way or another. Small-scale initiatives or a simple threat to withdraw political support can change behavior. What is of importance is that power be applied towards objectives that are common and not at cross purposes; that its application is based on a correct and shared analysis of what it will take to influence particular behaviors; and that leverage can be achieved through the ability to apply or withdraw carrots and sticks in a consistent and credible manner.

Preferably, Hard and Soft Power actors need to work towards a common objective. But as discussed, this can be challenging, and sometimes there are different objectives that are sought by different sources of power in the same environment. At a minimum, those sources of power cannot work at cross purposes. For the United States this can be a challenge in places where there are multiple U.S. objectives, and particularly if one of them will trump the others. For example, during the beginning of the Darfur crisis in 2003, the U.S. Government was pushing for the Sudanese Government to stop facilitating the violence and called on the international community to intervene and hold all parties accountable. At the same time, however, the United States was fighting the war on terror and was counting on the Government of Sudan to assist in that effort. This meant that the United States would only push the Sudanese Government so far in order not to lose that partnership. Thus, the United States had limited leverage in regards to Darfur. This is also why civilian and military coordination is so important. They work in the same forums with similar actors but may be seeking different objectives and inadvertently working at cross purposes.

When Soft and Hard Power Combine

Having understood what it takes for either Hard or Soft Power to be effective, we must examine what happens when the two are used simultaneously. The presence of Hard and Soft Power together can be incredibly advantageous but there is also a risk that leverage and influence can be more easily lost when the two are combined. This is the paradox of power: more types of power can mean amplified results or less impact. When applying Soft and Hard Power in the same environment, new obstacles arise for ensuring the components of effective power are present. What are these obstacles, and why does this happen? Certain factors in the environment lead to trends that can be observed when Soft and Hard Power are combined in the same environment.

The Greater the Number of Actors, the More Challenging the Consistency

A frequent complaint about places such as Vietnam, Afghanistan and Iraq, is that the results in those places do not correspond to the amount of resources invested by the United States. Power achieved through influencing change is not necessarily an issue of quantity, but rather of how resources are combined and used jointly to maintain the requirements of effective power. If Hard and Soft Power are not used together in a combined strategy and approach, then those elements of Hard and Soft Power can actually have lesser utility than if there had been fewer resources.

As the types and quantity of power tools increase, the actors behind them increase. Those actors are more likely to have different understandings of the problem set and its solution. This is the inevitable fog of war that translates in the broader context into a fog of bureaucracy. The more complex the systems and actors, the harder it is to maintain a common vision and understanding amongst them. As described earlier, in order for power to be effective, it first needs to be the correct type of action to induce the desired behaviors. But mind reading is difficult in any context, let alone a foreign one. Everyone tends to read an environment from their own perspective. For example, in Iraq, soldiers thought that workers cleaning up garbage at night as part of development projects were laying IEDs. The workers were cleaning at night simply because it was too hot to do so during the day. In this case, intentions were easily misunderstood and could lead to disastrous consequences.

Once Both Hard and Soft Power Assets Are Deployed, the Balance Might Not Be Correct

The amount of Hard and Soft Power assets used is dependent upon what will influence the actor, and what influences that actor can change quickly. It is challenging to ensure that the quantity and type of Hard and Soft Power resources are always appropriate. During a protracted conflict, the balance of Soft and Hard Power approaches may have to shift. In Iraq in 2003, the short-term goal of removing Saddam Hussein's regime required significant Hard Power approaches. The United States, however, neglected sufficient Soft Power approaches as it became apparent that Iraqis were experiencing a country where services and security were deteriorating. The demise of their leader was less important than their day-to-day reality. As a result, the United States recognized that services were a key aspect of what influenced people's perceptions and behaviors, and quickly deployed Soft Power assets towards addressing those issues.

Different Objectives Or Different Understanding of the Objectives

As explained earlier, power cannot be effective if it is applied based on a different or wrong understanding of the objectives that it tries to achieve. This becomes even trickier when you have Hard and Soft Power assets in an arena where actors are used to looking at problems from very different angles. U.S. troops in Afghanistan might be focused on the objective of reducing violence and will therefore prioritize anything that stops kinetic action. This may be effective in its own right, but if the objective is to stop the ability of Al-Qaeda to operate, Soft Power approaches might better address the ability of the Afghan Government to prevent Al-Qaeda from re-establishing a foothold and reducing tribal support for extremists. In other cases, the means may be as confused as the ends. U.S. troops frequently use civil affairs projects thinking that the development projects' objectives are an end in itself (a new road, a new school, provision of medical care, etc.) This overlooks the fact that the objective of the mission is never a new road or a new school. Instead, the objective is either to gain support or approval from the local population or reward local actors for behavior. Likewise, the projects may also be designed to create faith in the host nation government's ability to provide basic services. Thus, these types of projects have to be designed with the larger goals in mind. Therefore, a road that is built without local support may actually lead to less local support even if it achieves the infrastructure goals set out during the mission.

Complicating matters is that often the United States has a number of layered and (hopefully) mutually supporting objectives in a particular region. As discussed in the case of Sudan, Hard Power assets are frequently geared towards one type of objective while Soft Power assets are focused on others. They can have challenges when they arrive in the same arena together and the tactics required for each might work against each other.

More Actors Mean Less Time-Effective Interventions

Credibility is necessary for legitimacy and effective power. But as described earlier, timeliness is a key component of credibility. If actors do not act when they said they would or do not seize a moment where there is a window for influencing, then that moment can be lost. Worse, credibility is lost when this happens, which diminishes the ability of actors to have power in the future. But the more actors there are, the harder it is to act in a timely manner because everyone's actions should be coordinated with those of others, and some actors are slower than others, dragging the rest down with them. Also, coordination takes time and staff. It can require hours of meetings in order to come to mutual understandings to coordinate the application of those understandings. Indeed, while expected in the conduct of coalition operations, where—in the case of the NATO Alliance—every decision requires a 28 nation consensus—this sort of bureaucratic requirement for internal day-to-day decisions across both Hard and Soft Power assets, although frequently necessary, can be incapacitating.

The other challenge is unavailability of money or lack of bureaucratic processes to move things quickly. While a verbal promise can be made, it does not necessarily translate into action. For example, even though the United States might want to offer certain financial or development incentives to other countries, the timing may not work out. USAID (and many other parts of the U.S. Government) receives most of its funding once a year in the summer, and needs to commit it by the end of the fiscal year on September 30. This gives USAID only a three-month window to make decisions on programming. If an urgent political negotiation takes place in the Fall or Winter, the U.S. Mission in that country likely will not know its budget for that year, and will be limited in what it can offer until it knows its final budget and has the money in its hands. Even after it knows its budget (somewhere between the end of the calendar year and early into the next calendar year), promises can be made but the funds and resources will not flow until June or July, and sometimes August. This impedes timeliness.

Hard Power Will Frequently Trump Soft Power

When Hard and Soft Power are deployed in the same area, Hard Power tends to trump or overshadow Soft Power, which creates an imbalance in the application of various elements of power. Why does this happen? Firstly, Hard Power tends to be required in dire situations frequently related to security. As discussed in the Sudan example, security objectives tend to be prioritized over non-security objectives. But even when Soft Power resources are dedicated to addressing security issues, Hard Power will tends to trump. In the U.S. example, most Hard Power comes from the Department of Defense, whose systems are designed for speed and contain the required human, financial, and logistical resources to execute quickly. For good reason, the U.S. military has been trained to have a "get it done quickly no matter what" mentality. These are all important characteristics for deploying Hard Power, but the speed at which the Department of Defense wants to move can inhibit its success when they try to apply Soft Power. Non-kinetic forms of power usually take longer to execute. Although they could be physically executed just as quickly as Hard Power, Soft Power resources usually require local buy-in and can require implementation with or through local actors who work on slower timelines with limited resources. Frequently, the process of executing Soft Power assets is more important than the ultimate output metric. Hurrying or ignoring local buy-in to speed up the process can result in reduced or no influence at best, and a hostile environment at worst. Unlike the Department of Defense, Soft Power actors are used to having to take their time on certain issues. This requires patience, which can be challenging for Department of Defense actors whose nature is to focus on achieving tangible metrics in the shortest period of time possible.

U.S. Soft and Hard Power Objectives May Be the Same, But the Way to Achieve Them May Differ

Hard and Soft Power are frequently wielded by different types of actors with differing perspectives on issues and their solutions. For example, the Yemeni military might see military operations as the solution, while the Yemeni civilian government might see negotiations with key groups as the solution. But if these efforts are not coordinated or sequenced correctly, the military operations may turn away the groups that Soft Power elements of the government are trying to influence. As long as military operations upset the local population, Soft Power components may never be able to make headway on influencing the local population to reject militants. People will frequently turn to what they know as the solution, but sometimes what they know is not appropriate at a given time.

How Soft and Hard Power Can Equal Smart Power

In sum, the determining factor for whether Hard and Soft Power will be of benefit or detriment is whether the components for effective power are present. On their own, the components of effective power (an understanding of what behavior change is sought, a common and accurate understanding of what will encourage behavior change in a target audience, and the leverage to create that shift) are not overly complicated but require smart policy and deliberate execution. If these components for effective power are present, the application of Hard and Soft Power together faces additional challenges of time lags due to additional actors, misunderstandings and working at cross purposes due to difference in problem perception. But these challenges can be overcome, and when they are, Hard and Soft Power combined can be incredibly powerful by offering an array of tools for influence. During the Kosovo crisis, Hard Power through bombings demonstrated to Milosevic the seriousness of U.S. commitment to protecting ethnic Albanians while using Soft Power elements to influence the political negotiations. In Yemen and Pakistan, drones, and Pakistani and Yemeni military operations have been combined with Soft Power elements to reduce militant influences. The threat of force can sometimes be enough and brings credibility to Soft Power's influence. It can change the political calculus in a way for Soft Power to be more effective and possibly remove the need to execute Hard Power.

As the Obama Administration moves into its second term and resources are scant while requirements for power and influence are high, the administration should look at a few methods to ensure that Smart Power is a net gain. This includes keeping requirements for power in mind when making policy decisions and providing clear policy guidance from the National Security Council to minimize infighting and misunderstandings combined with decentralization of decision-making at the country-level. The need to coordinate Soft and Hard Power resources has been recognized as a requirement. But instead of finding streamlined ways to coordinate, additional bureaucratic coordination has tended to be the solution. Hyper-coordination is the death of effective Smart Power. Coordination is necessary, and all Hard and Soft Power assets should be coordinated through the U.S. embassy (which is not always the case). But requiring the coordination of the minutiae, often at headquarters rather than in the field, is time consuming and unnecessary. More importantly, it affects the credibility behind the Soft and Hard Power efforts because it slows them down. Timing and responsiveness are necessary for credibility, and to ensure that the right power resources are applied at the right time and not too late.

Additionally, the United States should broaden its interpretation of Hard and Soft Power assets at its disposal (which was incorporated in the Quadrennial Diplomacy and Development Review). Frequently, the United States has looked to itself for Hard Power, but it should also use Soft Power assets to influence other actors to apply their own

Hard Power assets in a way that supports U.S. objectives. This can include providing Soft Power assets to train other actors in how to improve their Hard Power capabilities, as the U.S. did in the Philippines and Colombia by training militaries to tackle objectives that are of mutual interest. This Hard Power through proxy still allows for the influence that Hard Power brings while reducing risk, political obstacles and the costs of deployment of U.S. Hard Power assets.

Smart Power is about defining what ingredients need to be used, how many of them, and to what end. Smart Power requires understanding the ultimate objective, what behavior changes are required to achieve that objective, and what Hard and Soft Power assets would encourage that behavior. It is about looking at the objective, what it will take to achieve that objective, and ensuring that all actors understand and work towards that objective in addition to warranting leverage. Clear guidance on objectives and decentralized streamlined coordination across all Soft and Hard Power assets are required to ensure consistency and credibility. Although the Quadrennial Diplomacy and Development Review (QDDR) provides the objectives that the United States is trying to achieve, it does not outline the underlying policies and tactics that are required for those objectives to be obtained. These policies and tactics should be determined by the U.S. Government elements in each country. Clearer objectives and policies for how these objectives will be obtained will ensure that Hard and Soft Power assets combined are a net gain rather than the Achilles tendon.

In the future, the U.S. Government should fight against creating additional coordination bureaucracy and seek ways to simplify the number of actors to be coordinated. The number of actors contributing to Soft and Hard Power assets overseas has been growing exponentially over the last twenty years. This has happened partly due to agencies wanting to expand their portfolios (and therefore, their budgets). It is also the result of the push for "whole of government" efforts overseas, which was a good interim measure since Hard and Soft Power assets were sprinkled across the U.S. Government. "Whole of government" efforts, however, are laborious and challenging given the number of actors who are currently involved in applying Hard and Soft Power assets overseas. (For example, at one point, there were more than 20 agencies who worked on international policy) The U.S. Government should streamline responsibilities for tasks overseas within fewer agencies and offices, and ensure that they report through a central mechanism. In regards to Soft Power assets, currently, only USAID, State, and the Millenium Challenge Account jointly plan and report while many other U.S. Government actors continue to operate outside of these channels. It will be challenging to remove some of the international portfolios from some U.S. Government organizations because no agency wants to lose its resources, but it will make the U.S. Government more streamlined, facilitating coordination of Hard and Soft Power resources. This will ultimately result in a U.S. Government that effectively wields both its Hard and Soft Power assets such that each is successful on its own, and when combined, exponentially more powerful.

Part II

The U.S.-EU Smart Power Couple

Chapter 4

Smart Power and Multilateral Diplomacy

Esther Brimmer

The concept of Smart Power entered the policy and academic mainstream nearly a decade ago in response to perceptions of an excessive reliance on Hard Power tools, and particularly the use of force by the United States without sanction by the international community. Early proponents of "Smart Power" argued that national interests, including those of the United States, would be best and more sustainably achieved through a balance of Soft Power (traditional diplomacy, people-to-people exchange, trade, cultural interaction, etc.) and the more martial tools associated with Hard Power.

Over the subsequent decade, the variable definitions of Smart Power have evolved to reflect a rapidly changing foreign affairs landscape—a landscape shaped increasingly by transnational issues and what can only be described as truly global challenges. Nations of the world must now calibrate their foreign policy investments to try to leverage new opportunities while protecting their interests from emerging vulnerabilities. Smart Power is no longer an alternative path; it is a four-lane imperative.

The world in 2014 is fundamentally different from previous periods, growing vastly more interconnected, interdependent, networked, and complex. National economies are in many cases inextricably intertwined, with cross-border imports and exports increasing nearly tenfold over the past forty years, and more than doubling over just the past decade. At the same time, we are all connected—and connected immediately—to news and events that in past generations would have been restricted to their local vicinities.

Consider, for example, the 2011 tsunami that devastated parts of Japan. Not only did we know in real time of the earthquake that trig-

At the time of writing Dr. Brimmer was Assistant Secretary for the Bureau of International Organization Affairs at the United States Department of State. She wishes to thank Christopher Le Mon and Mark Schlachter for their assistance.

gered the tsunami, we had live coverage of some of the tsunami's most devastating impacts and then round-the-clock coverage of the Fukushima nuclear power plant crisis. Communications technology brings such events to us without delay and in high definition. This communications revolution, headlined by the explosion of social media, carries with it the almost unlimited potential to inform and educate. It also provides people and communities with new ability to influence and advance their causes—both benevolent and otherwise, as the dramatic events of recent years in North Africa and the Middle East have made clear.

At the same time, global power is more diffuse today than in centuries. Although predictions of the nation-state's demise have gone unrealized, non-state actors—including NGOs, corporations, and international organizations—are more influential today than perhaps at any point in human history. The same might be said for transnational criminal networks and other harmful actors. Concurrently, we are witnessing the rise of new centers of influence—the so-called "emerging" nations—that are seeking and gaining positions of global leadership. These emerging powers bring unique histories and new perspectives to the discussion of current challenges and the future of global governance. Several of these countries are democracies and share many of the core values of the United States; others have sharply different political systems and perspectives. *All* are gauging how to be more active in the global arena.

It is this new, more diffused global system that must now find means of addressing today's pressing global challenges—challenges that in many cases demand Smart Power ingenuity.

From terrorism to nuclear proliferation, climate change to pandemic disease, transnational crime to cyber attacks, violations of fundamental human rights to natural disasters, today's most urgent security challenges pay no heed to state borders.

So, just as global power is more diffuse, so too are the opposing threats and challenges, and it is in this new reality that the United States must define and employ its Smart Power resources. That reality demands a definition that must now far exceed the origin parameters of hard and soft. Many of these challenges would be unresponsive to traditional Hard tools (coercion, economic sanctions, military force), while the application of Soft tools (norm advancement, cultural influence, public diplomacy) in customary channels is likely to provide unsatisfactory impact.

Ultimately, the other component necessary in today's Smart Power alchemy is robust, focused, and sustained international cooperation. In effect, in an increasing number of instances, Smart Power must now feature shared power, and in that context foreign policy choices must follow two related but distinct axes.

First, those policy choices must strengthen a state's overall stature and influence (rather than diminish it), leaving the state undertaking the action in a position of equal or greater global standing. This is easier said than done. The proliferation in challenges facing *all* states has created a need for multiple, simultaneous diplomatic transactions among a broadening cast of actors. Given the nature of today's threats facing states both large and small, those transactions have never been more frequent and at times overlapping—a reality that requires new agility and synchronization within foreign policy hierarchies. States that are less capable of responding to this new reality may experience diminished political capital and international standing by acting on contemporary threats in isolation or without a full appreciation of the reigning international sentiment. Many observers have highlighted U.S. decision-making in advance of the 2003 Iraq invasion as indicative of just this phenomenon.

Alternatively, states applying a new Smart Power approach to their foreign policy recognize the overlapping need to maintain global standing and stature while seeking resolution of individual policy challenges. We see considerable effort on the part of emerging powers to find just that balance, and I would argue that the United States has also made great strides in that regard since 2009.

Second, Smart Power policy choices must contribute to the strength and resilience of the international system. As noted above, the globalization of contemporary challenges and security threats has augmented the need for effective cooperation among states and other international actors, and placed even greater demands on the global network of international institutions, conferences, frameworks, and groupings in which these challenges are more and more frequently addressed. Given this heightened need for structures to facilitate international collaboration, states are more rarely undertaking foreign policy courses of action that entirely lack a multilateral component, or that feature no interaction with or demands upon the international architecture. As recent American history shows, even states with unilateral tendencies have found themselves returning to the multilateral fold to address aspects of a threat or challenge that simply cannot be addressed effectively alone.

Upon assuming office, President Obama took bold steps to respond to the new global realities described above, and to reinvigorate U.S. multilateral diplomacy accordingly. Over the last four years, it has become increasingly clear that effective multilateral diplomacy can create the conditions for an international response to a global challenge or threat that is greater than the sum of its national parts, and that contributes to the effective resolution of both the instant challenge and future ones. Stemming from the assessment noted at the outset—that evolution in global threats and devolutions of international clout had fundamentally changed the nature of contemporary power—the U.S. expanded even upon its traditionally active role within the United Nations, affirming its centrality to U.S. foreign policy. Indeed, although action through the United Nations is far from the sole policy tool utilized by the United States, few U.S. foreign policy challenges—whether primary or secondary in importance—find themselves advanced without significant action in UN bodies by the United States.

Take, for example, the President's controversial decision that the United States should seek election to the UN Human Rights Council. That controversy stemmed from the fact that the Council was only the slightest improvement over its predecessor, the justifiably maligned Human Rights *Commission*. The Council was launched with great fanfare, but then quickly reverted to bad habits—protecting despots and serial human rights abusers, and reserving unique and corrosive attention for one UN member state—Israel. Seeking and winning election in 2009 was a risk for the United States, but it was a risk rooted in the President's determination to reinvest in UN bodies that could be improved through vigorous U.S. engagement.

That risk has paid off. Yes, the Council continues to frustrate on issues related to Israel, and too comfortably accommodates illegitimate voices on human rights issues. Nonetheless, the ledger is clearly in the black over the last four years, with dramatic and positive Council action on freedoms of expression and assembly; Lesbian, Gay, Bisexual, and Transgender (LGBT) rights; and persistent focus on violators of universal human rights worldwide, including in Iran, Syria, Sudan, North Korea, Cote d'Ivoire, Cambodia, Belarus, Sri Lanka, and Eritrea. We achieved this progress by recognizing and responding to the very realities discussed above. We sought and found common ground between both our traditional allies and more uncommon partners. We spoke loudly and resolutely, but were willing to speak in chorus with international voices. This new approach did not necessarily mean the absence of differences, but it did mean that over time the United States strengthened its credibility and standing on the Council and the stature of the Council itself. That, in turn, was apparent in the U.S. re-election to the Council in 2012, an election in which the United States received the largest number of votes on its regional slate.

Take also the example of food security. In the wake of food price crises in 2007 and 2008, the United States and G8 partner countries recognized the need for a new kind of collaboration on food issues— collaboration designed to reshape the global approach to ensuring long-term food security. At the 2009 L'Aquila G8 Summit, action was taken to improve coordination, support country-owned processes and plans, and strengthen multilateral institutions to advance existing efforts to promote food security worldwide. That strengthening effort has included revitalizing FAO's Committee on Food Security to become more inclusive, more transparent, and more responsive to enduring needs. In a Smart Power context, this effort means seizing new opportunities to leverage partner nations, encourage engagement by emerging powers such as Brazil, and bolstering U.S. credibility as the largest supporter of international food relief and agricultural development activities.

Across the international system, the United States is actively and substantively engaged. We mark a similar effort by other developed and developing nations, as governments begin to come to terms with the new global reality. But, how do we measure the success or shortcomings of this new Smart Power era? The relative strength and effectiveness of international bodies may be evidence of deepening member state interest in both. Less measurable, perhaps, will be the relative influence of those nations following this new path and whether that influence can be sustained. For the United States, the simultaneous application of resources to traditional bilateral interaction will continue. In many ways, this bilateral capacity provides the United States with an important advantage in international fora. However, gone are the days when we can rely solely upon conversations in capitals to protect and promote our global priorities, just as most countries have little choice but to apply their more limited resources to collaborative bodies such as the UN.

The United States has invested heavily in restoring our stature and influence in the international system, while concurrently renewing and strengthening our commitment to that system itself. These investments come with frustrations, setbacks, and false starts. However, they are returning dividends in ways both obvious and incremental. In the UN General Assembly, that investment has meant building new coalitions on important resolutions, including highlighting the abysmal human rights records of Iran, North Korea, and Cuba. It also means revisiting our own voting decisions and, where possible and appropriate, shaping or joining global consensus. These twin efforts have resulted in a dramatic shift in our voting coincidence with other countries, diminishing our isolation in the General Assembly and strengthening coalitions for future action. That coincidence (on voted resolutions) found its low in 2007 (18%), but has subsequently risen above 50% (2011). This alone is not proof enough of a return on our Smart Power investment, but is one indicator that such returns warrant the diplomatic investment.

Chapter 5

The Most Effective Strategies: Looking at a Silver Bullet or Seeking Greater Energy Security?

Paula J. Dobriansky and Paul J. Saunders

All human activity requires energy—and the more energy one has, the more one can do. As a result, energy has been a central element of national power throughout history.

In the distant past, building Egypt's pyramids, Rome's vast network of roads, and China's Great Wall required enormous biological energy—food to support populations that could supply the massive labor force necessary for these early mega-projects. In a sense, the slow emergence of agricultural technologies that underlay these three empires, and many others, was the first energy revolution. The considerable energy that went in to each of these undertakings still captures the imagination; in fact, these impressive expenditures of energy have come to symbolize the civilizations that produced them.

Centuries later, the steam engine and the industrial revolution created the first modern empire—the British Empire—and sustained it across more than a century. While the British Empire still endured, the transition from coal to oil fueled America's emergence as a global power. Impressive oil and natural gas resources likewise played an essential role in the temporary successes of America's superpower rival, the Soviet Union, which fell apart when its domestic economic policies and the subsidy-driven Soviet bloc proved unsustainable in the face of collapsing energy prices.

Today, new oil and gas extraction technologies are reshaping global markets and may well alter both realities and perceptions of international power. Reduced U.S. natural gas imports have already affected Europe's energy markets and forced Russia's Gazprom to issue substantial refunds to its European customers. More changes could lie ahead for both the United States and Europe, creating new opportunities but also posing new challenges and dilemmas in transatlantic relations. It is thus a timely moment to assess the relationship between power and energy and to consider the implications of these new developments for the United States and its closest partners.

Power and Energy

There are many definitions of power in international relations, but most describe it as a nation's ability to compel or influence other nations to do something that they would not otherwise do. In practice, this can also mean a nation's ability to prevent others from doing something they would otherwise do. Smart power usually refers to the efficient selection among power's many tools—military, economic, diplomatic, cultural, or moral, to name only a few—and it is "smart" because its efficiency allows for greater leverage at lower cost. To be "smart" in the fullest sense of the word, however, smart power should minimize not only direct costs to those who exercise it, but also the indirect costs of potential unintended consequences.

In the period since the 1973 Organization of Petroleum Exporting Countries (OPEC) embargo on the United States, which quadrupled the price of oil, Americans have been understandably unaccustomed to viewing their nation as one possessing considerable energy power. To the contrary, most Americans have seen their country as unacceptably vulnerable to the vagaries of the global oil market, which drove the oil prices to disruptive lows in the 1980s before sending them to punishing heights in the first decade of the twenty-first century. Nevertheless, the United States was an important energy power for much of the fossil fuel era. Only after World War II did America become a net importer of petroleum products; its net imports of natural gas remained minimal for another twenty years or more.

Unsurprisingly, energy and access to energy have been deeply intertwined with U.S. foreign policy for much of this period. When confronted with Japan's expansionist conduct in Asia, America cut off its oil supplies—some 80% of Japan's consumption—in the summer of 1941 to apply pressure on Tokyo. (Of course, Japan in turn sought to end the U.S. embargo by breaking the back of the U.S. Navy in its attack on Pearl Harbor.) A little more than a decade later, reacting to Iran's nationalization of its oil industry, Washington played a central role in organizing the 1953 coup that brought down the country's elected government and installed Shah Mohammed Reza Pahlavi. In 1980, after the Soviet invasion of Afghanistan, President Jimmy Carter announced America's determination to use force if necessary to maintain secure access to global markets for Middle East energy, a policy now known as the Carter Doctrine—and a major consideration in the 1990-91 war to expel Iraq from Kuwait. Today, the U.S. has mobilized international support for sanctions on Iran's energy sector, and an embargo on its exports, in an effort to discourage Tehran from developing nuclear weapons. Since Russia's annexation of Crimea, many have called for sanctions on Russia's energy sector and for U.S. natural gas exports to Europe in order to reduce its dependence on Russian gas supplies.

Of course, America's "energy power" is not limited to oil and natural gas and its energy-related foreign policy decisions have not been driven solely by its overseas pursuit of these two resources. Plentiful cheap coal was a key facilitator of the industrialization and electrification that made America a superpower; it underpins U.S. foreign policy. Nuclear energy and its inseparable alter ego—the nuclear warhead—have been central to U.S. power and policy since their development; President Dwight Eisenhower's Atoms for Peace initiative was simultaneously an effort to promote nuclear energy and to embarrass the Soviet Union. More recently, Washington has used the prospect of civil nuclear cooperation as a carrot in relations with Russia and Middle Eastern nations. Conversely, solar power, and wind technologies and markets are an area of intense U.S.-China economic competition—and among the sources of tension due to disagreements over intellectual property rights, government subsidies, and cyber-espionage.

Moreover, while analysts and commentators commonly assess "power" in the energy sphere by measuring oil and gas reserves, production, and exports, large advanced economies like America's can also derive a form of power from their roles as major consumers.

Sources of America's Energy Power

A deeper understanding of America's international energy power requires a more detailed assessment of the resources, capabilities, and instruments at Washington's disposal across its energy sector. We will first examine U.S. energy sources: fossil fuels, nuclear power, and other forms of renewable energy.

The shale gas boom is one of the most visible changes in America's energy sector. Dramatic increases in natural gas production facilitated by horizontal drilling and hydraulic fracturing have had a profound impact on the United States and seem likely to continue to do so unless producers experience a major environmental disaster or some other serious and unexpected problem. According to a recent study by the global information and analysis firm IHS, shale gas supported 600,000 jobs in the United States in 2010, a number projected to reach 870,000 in 2015 and 1.6 million in 2035, when shale gas would account for 60% of U.S. natural gas production.[1] The study predicts that this will add $118 billion per year to the U.S. economy by 2015 and $231 billion per year by 2035—and that the cumulative tax revenues for federal, state, and local governments could approach $1 trillion during this period.

At the international level, the United States will likely become a net exporter of natural gas not long after 2020, according to the U.S. Energy Information Administration.[2] Due in part to legislative limits on U.S. natural gas exports, from 2009–2012 domestic natural gas prices were roughly half the peak price levels in 2005–2008, though prices are now somewhat higher.[3]

Thanks to new technologies, U.S. oil production appears to be increasing on a trajectory comparable to that of U.S. natural gas. IHS projects that new approaches to extracting "tight oil" could generate 1.3 million new jobs, $988 billion in economic impact, and $97 billion in tax revenue.[4] Moreover, the International Energy Agency (IEA)

---

[1] "Shale Gas Predicted to Support Nearly 870,000 Jobs," http://press.ihs.com/press-release/energy-power/shale-gas-supports-more-600000-american-jobs-today-2015-shale-gas-predict (last accessed: July 1st, 2014).

[2] *Annual Energy Outlook 2012 with Projections to 2035*, Energy Information Administration, www.eia.gov/forecasts/aeo/pdf/0383(2012).pdf#page75 (last accessed: July 1st, 2014) See Figure 106, p. 92.

[3] *The Annual Energy Outlook 2012*, prepared by the U.S. Energy Information Administration is available on the EIA website at www.eia.gov/forecasts/aeo (last accessed: July 1st, 2014).

[4] Stephen Trammel, "Tight Oil Turning Around U.S. Oil Industry," www.ihs.com/products/oil-gas-information/source-newsletter/us/jan2012/tight-oil-turning-industry.aspx (last accessed: July 1st, 2014).

estimates that the United States could become the world's largest oil producer around 2020, surpassing Saudi Arabia (until Saudi production again overtakes America's in the mid-2020s). The IEA also foresees the United States becoming a net oil exporter by 2030, though America will continue to import significant amounts of specific petroleum products.[5]

The United States has long been an energy power in coal, with some 260 billion tons of coal reserves according to the U.S. Energy Information Administration (EIA), amounting to more than one-quarter of global coal reserves. America is the second-largest producer and the second-largest consumer of coal; China mines and uses coal at nearly four times the U.S. rate of approximately 1 billion tons per year. Due to its high consumption of coal, however, the U.S. is only the fourth largest exporter, behind Indonesia, Australia and Russia.[6]

Since America has abundant coal supplies, few in the United States have considered coal to be a strategic resource like oil or natural gas. In fact, as a practical matter, few Americans outside coal-producing regions probably think about coal at all outside the context of its environmental impacts. Despite this, extensive U.S. coal supplies have historically contributed very substantially to the country's economic growth, and by extension to its international leadership. Today, however, rapid increases in natural gas production and decreases in prices have encouraged a major shift from coal to natural gas in U.S. electricity generation. Of course, as part of its strategy to combat climate change, the Obama administration is seeking to further discourage coal use through Environmental Protection Agency regulation of carbon dioxide emissions. The United States and other nations have also been seeking to develop affordable clean coal technologies.

The U.S. has a similarly leading role in nuclear power as the world's largest operator of commercial nuclear power plants, with a fleet of 104 reactors—nearly one-quarter of the global total—in 2012.[7] Amer-

[5]European Investment Bank, "Energy Lending Criteria," published July 25, 2013, http://www.eib.org/attachments/strategies/eib_energy_lending_criteria_en.pdf (last accessed: July 1st, 2014).
[6]Coal statistics are drawn from the Energy Information Administration's web site, www.eia.gov. See country data at www.eia.gov/countries/data.cfm (last accessed: July 1st, 2014).
[7]"Nuclear Power Reactors in the World", International Atomic Energy Agency (Vienna, 2012).

ica's nuclear power plants produce roughly 20% of its electricity, but nuclear power has a wider impact on the country's international leadership. For example, according to the Nuclear Energy Institute, a leading industry group, the commercial nuclear sector employs some 120,000 people, many of whom are highly trained engineers and technicians.[8] Additional personnel work in government nuclear programs, especially in the U.S. Department of Energy, which oversees nuclear energy and manages the nation's nuclear weapons complex, and in academic research. There are 42 operational research reactors in the United States, about one-sixth of the global total.[9]

The U.S. nuclear power industry stagnated after the 1979 Three Mile Island accident, which fed public concern over nuclear safety and complicated efforts to finance and build new reactors. The Energy Policy Act of 2005 sought to stimulate new development of nuclear power in America, largely in order to diversify electricity generation at a time of relatively high natural gas prices. Progress was slow, however, and appears to have stalled again in the wake of Japan's 2011 earthquake and tsunami, which caused a major accident and radiation release at the Fukushima Daiichi nuclear plant. Lower natural gas prices in the United States have also undermined the economic competitiveness of nuclear power in America.

Natural gas prices have likewise posed a challenge to the development of renewable energy, which comprised only 9.4% of America's total primary energy consumption in 2011.[10] Of this, biomass makes up nearly half the total, hydroelectric power another third while wind amounts to one-eighth of all renewable energy consumption.[11] In 2010, the United States was the third-largest producer of renewable

---

[8]"Nuclear Industry's Comprehensive Approach Develops Skilled Work Force for the Future," http://www.nei.org/corporatesite/media/filefolder/Nuclear_Industrys_Comprehensive_Approach_Devlops_Skilled_Work_Force_for_the_Future_Sept_2010.pdf (last accessed: July 1st, 2014).

[9]The International Atomic Energy Agency maintains a searchable database of research reactors at http://www-ns.iaea.org/tech-areas/research-reactor-safety/irsrr-home.asp?s=2&l=15 (last accessed: July 1st, 2014). Russia's massive nuclear complex includes some sixty-five operational research reactors—no other nation maintains more than the United States.

[10]See the U.S. Energy Information Administration's overview at www.eia.gov/totalenergy/data/annual/showtext.cfm?t=ptb0103 (last accessed: July 1st, 2014).

[11]See www.eia.gov/totalenergy/data/annual/pdf/sec10_3.pdf (last accessed: July 1st, 2014). Solar energy is just 1.7% of the renewable total and therefore a vanishingly small share of America's overall energy mix.

electricity, behind China (whose output is nearly double that of the United States) and Brazil.[12]

From a policy perspective, the United States has tended to focus on subsidizing uncompetitive renewable technologies in the hope that a larger market share will reduce costs and lead to wider adoption. Still, the United States is a leader in many areas, such as battery research. (Efficient storage is essential for renewable energy sources with variable output, such as solar and wind power, and also has a major impact on electric vehicles and in other areas.)

America in the World

Assessing the international environment in which the United States and its allies will operate in the coming one to two decades is a challenging task. Even from the narrow perspective of global energy markets and their impact on the international system, evolving technologies and trade patterns make this quite difficult. Nevertheless, informed speculation can be helpful in understanding the possibilities and formulating broad options and plans.

In assessing the wider implications of America's possible emergence as a fossil fuel superpower, three regions appear most important. The first, Europe, is home to America's closest international partners and a major force in international security and economic affairs. Asia is the world's most dynamic region; many see its leading economic power, China, as a rising global power. The Middle East is of course a major source of both energy and instability.

While it is tempting to address each of these three regions separately, as a practical matter it is quite difficult to do so—particularly in the world of energy, where both Russia and the Middle East not only lie between Europe and Asia but are intimately interconnected with each due to their roles as major energy exporters. With this in mind, the two following sections will focus on oil and gas in the Europe-Russia-Asia and Europe-Middle East-Asia triangles. A third section

---

[12]See www.eia.gov/cfapps/ipdbproject/iedindex3.cfm?tid=6&pid=29&aid=12 (last accessed: July 1st, 2014).

will cover nuclear, coal, and renewable energies, which differ in important respects from oil and gas.

Europe, Russia and Asia

The shale gas revolution in the United States has already had significant—and mixed—effects within the context of transatlantic relations. On the one hand, decreased U.S. natural gas imports have put downward pressure on the prices that the Russian gas monopoly Gazprom can charge its European customers, who now enjoy greater access to liquefied natural gas (LNG) from the Middle East that had been previously intended for the United States. As a result of this and due to slow European economies, Gazprom's gas sales to Europe declined from 156 billion cubic meters (bcm) in 2011 to 151 bcm in 2012 even as the company returned $3.4 billion to customers in compensation for its relatively high pricing.[13] If these changes are sustained, Europe's gas consumers will benefit from greater diversity of supply as well as lower costs. However, some Middle East energy initially diverted to Europe has since entered more profitable markets in Asia.

Nevertheless, Europe's natural gas prices remain well above those in the United States. According to press reports, this four-fold gap is already encouraging some energy intensive industries to locate new manufacturing in the United States rather than Europe, particularly in the chemicals sector, where natural gas is both a power source and a raw material. Germany's BASF has invested $5.7 billion in the United States since 2009, worrying some of its Europe-based workers.[14]

Looking ahead, the future of Russia's energy sector could have significant implications for European security and prosperity—and shale gas could have important consequences for Russia. Russia's federal government currently earns 50% of its total revenues from taxes and duties on the country's oil and natural gas production, up from 20% a

---

[13]"Gazprom Profits Slide 10% on Lower Gas Sales," Charles Clover, *Financial Times*, April 30, 2013.

[14]"European Industry Flocks to U.S. to Take Advantage of Cheaper Gas," Michael Birnbaum, *The Washington Post*, April 1, 2013, http://www.washingtonpost.com/world/europe/european-industry-flocks-to-cheap-us-gas/2013/04/01/454d06ea-8a2c-11e2-98d9-3012c1cd8d1e_story.html (last accessed: July 1st, 2014).

decade ago.[15] Moreover, growth in this revenue has supported increased spending on a variety of social causes. As a result, any significant and sustained reduction in energy prices can ultimately become a danger to the country's economic and social stability. Russia is more vulnerable to oil prices than to natural gas prices, but new gas supplies appear to be restraining growth in oil prices as well.

Russian officials and Gazprom have long sought to raise additional revenue for the state and the company and to gain new leverage in dealing with European customers by developing substantial natural gas exports to China. They may have succeeded with a key bilateral energy agreement that could see $400 billion in gas deliveries over 30 years beginning in 2018. Gazprom appears to have made some price concessions to secure the long-awaited deal during Putin's May 2014 visit to Beijing. Nevertheless, the financing for the massive capital investments needed to make the deal a reality remains unclear.

Further, Russia's energy firms cannot discount China's enormous shale gas reserves in the future. According to the EIA, China may have shale gas reserves even greater than those in the United States.[16] Should Beijing come close to self-sufficiency in natural gas in the foreseeable future, it could further weaken Gazprom's ability to maintain existing price levels for its exports to Europe and limit its long-term opportunities for expansion.

Moreover, Ukraine and to a lesser extent Poland also have notable shale gas reserves (though efforts to develop these resources in Poland have stumbled). While limited in comparison to U.S. or Chinese deposits, they are quite respectable relative to natural gas consumption in the two countries, and some of their immediate neighbors, who are currently highly dependent on gas imports from Russia. In the Ukrainian case, 3.6 trillion cubic meters in unproved shale gas

---

[15]*Public Debt Management Policy of the Russian Federation for 2013-2015*, Government of the Russian Federation, http://www.minfin.ru/common/img/uploaded/library/2012/12/ public_debt_policy_of_the_russian_federation_in_2013-2015_final_2.pdf p. 8 (last accessed: July 1st, 2014).

[16]"China Must Exploit Its Shale Gas," Elizabeth Muller, *The New York Times*, www.nytimes.com/2013/04/13/opinion/china-must-exploit-its-shale-gas.html?_r=0 (last accessed: July 1st, 2014). See also *World Shale Gas Resources: An Initial Assessment of 14 Regions Outside the United States*, www.eia.gov/analysis/studies/worldshalegas/ (last accessed: July 1st, 2014).

reserves could replace all of its current imports from Russia as well as those of Poland, the Czech Republic, Hungary, Bulgaria and Romania for over 50 years. Alternatively, Ukraine could replace only its own imports for about 90 years.[17] Of course, developing these resources will not be easy or automatic and each nation faces constraints in areas like infrastructure, the legal/regulatory environment, public opinion, and availability of the massive quantities of water needed for the fracking process. That said, the Ukraine crisis seems to have strengthened political support for energy development.

Taking into account these possible impacts, it is perhaps unsurprising that top Russian officials and energy executives have consistently downplayed shale gas and its future role in energy markets. Russian President Vladimir Putin has stressed its "much higher" production costs and "serious environmental problems"[18] while Gazprom CEO Alexey Miller claimed in early 2013 that "none of the wells [in the United States] has a positive value" and that shale gas "is a bubble that will burst soon."[19]

Vladimir Putin, however, has more recently acknowledged some of the difficulties that America's shale gas boom has posed for Moscow, including growth of the market for LNG, which is global rather than regional and pipeline-based. At a recent meeting of the Gas Exporting Countries Forum in Moscow, he said that the growing globalization of the gas market "increases pressure on the exporting countries" and that "attempts to dictate terms of pipeline gas supplies that are economically unacceptable to producers," "to change the principles of gas supplies on the basis of long-term contracts, to detach contract prices from the value of oil and petroleum products" are "a serious challenge for all of us here."[20]

---

[17] The figure cited is for unproved technically recoverable reserves. See "Technically Recoverable Shale Oil and Shale Gas Resources: An Assessment of 137 Shale Formations in 41 Countries Outside the United States," U.S. Energy Information Administration, June 10, 2013, Table 3.

[18] See "Direct Line with Vladimir Putin," April 25, 2013, http://eng.kremlin.ru/news/5328 (last accessed: July 1st, 2014) and "Meeting of the Commission for Strategic Development of the Fuel and Energy Sector and Environmental Security," October 23, 2012.

[19] "Russian Gas Flow Can't Be Reversed from Europe to Ukraine – Gazprom," March 30, 2013, www.itar-tass.com/en/c32/692009.html (last accessed: July 1st, 2014).

[20] "Summary: Putin Urges Retention of Basic Principles in Long-Term Gas Contracts," Interfax, July 2, 2013.

As an exporter, Russia is keenly interested in maintaining long-term stability of demand and revenue from its European customers, both of which are undermined as the size of spot markets for LNG relative to pipeline gas grows.

From this perspective, a $20 billion deal between Gazprom and a consortium of Japanese firms to build a LNG plant and other facilities to export up to 10 million tons per year of Russian gas to Japan and elsewhere in Asia may reflect an additional effort by the company to hedge against uncertain market prospects in Europe and China. President Vladimir Putin, and then-Prime Minister Yoshihiko Noda, personally signed the agreement at the 2012 APEC Summit in Vladivostok and also announced that Noda would likely visit Russia before the end of the year—though this did not take place due to Noda's departure from office. Putin is now set to visit Japan in fall 2014; one key question is whether Japan and Japanese companies will be as firm in price talks as their European and Chinese counterparts have been. Japan's ongoing energy crisis following the Fukushima nuclear accident may make this difficult.

More generally, if Russian officials determine that their nation faces a serious economic threat from increasing shale gas production in the United States or elsewhere, they will very likely seek avenues to respond to and to limit the risk. In Central Europe, this could include Russian efforts to acquire or block projects to potentially competing pipelines. President Putin's remarks at the international conference cited above make clear that Moscow is attempting to build political support among traditional gas exporters to resist possible changes in international markets.

Europe, the Middle East and Asia

The combination of America's new energy wealth with the Obama Administration's "pivot" to Asia—more recently termed a "rebalancing"—has led many to speculate that the United States might "withdraw" from the Middle East and give up on the region's frustrating if not intractable problems. While the reasons behind this thinking are understandable, particularly at a time when Washington has struggled to find a formula for leadership there without excessive reliance on its hard power, the United States will continue to have compelling national interests at stake in the Middle East and is unlikely to ignore it.

Many factors will encourage Washington's continued engagement in the Middle East. At the broadest level, the region remains a source of multiple serious security challenges, including Iran's nuclear ambitions, tension between Israel and the Palestinians, a civil war in Syria during which government forces appear to have employed chemical weapons, and widespread political and social uncertainty following the "Arab Spring." Each of these can have significant international implications for the United States.

More narrowly, even if America eventually exports more natural gas and oil than it imports, it will likely continue to import natural gas as well as certain types of oil best suited to U.S. refineries and needs. Since oil in particular is globally traded, the United States will remain vulnerable to oil-price volatility both directly and indirectly through its effects on the international economy. According to the EIA, America used an average 18,949,000 barrels of oil per day in 2011[21], or nearly 7 billion barrels for the year. At that level of consumption, a $5-per-barrel increase in the price of oil would cost America approximately $35 billion, more than the U.S. Congress appropriated to the Department of Energy in 2011.[22] Security and stability in the Middle East will matter to America and Americans.

At the same time, almost all of America's closest allies—including many in NATO as well as Japan and South Korea—will remain highly dependent on Middle East energy, Middle East security, or both. As of 2009, Eurostat estimated that the EU-27 countries depended on oil imports for 83.5% of consumption.[23] As of 2011, approximately one-third of Europe's oil imports come from the Middle East and North Africa.[24] European efforts to reduce natural gas imports from Russia

---

[21]See www.eia.gov/countries/index.cfm?topL=con (last accessed: July 1st, 2014).

[22]The "base appropriation" in 2011 was $29.9 billion; see Fiscal Year 2011 Summary of Performance and Financial Information, http://energy.gov/sites/prod/files/fy11SumRpt.pdf (last accessed: July 1st, 2014).

[23]See: the United Nations Conference on Trade and Development's report, "Trade and Development Report 2012", United Nations publications, 2012.

[24]See the European Commission's Market Observatory and Statistics reports, Monthly and cumulated Crude Oil Imports (volumes and prices) by EU and non EU country, "Registration of Crude Oil Imports and Deliveries in the European Union (EU27), 2011.

are likely increase the EU's gas dependence on Middle East exporters. And Japan is even more dependent upon the Middle East, relying upon the region for some 87% of its oil imports. Moreover, Japan is almost wholly dependent upon imports for its oil consumption.[25]

America's allies are not the only major economies to depend upon Middle East energy. According to the U.S. Energy Information Administration, China imported 56% of its oil, of which 51% originated in the Middle East.[26] By 2035, the EIA expects China to import 75% of its crude oil; Beijing is likely to depend even more heavily on Middle East exporters by that time. Taking into account the tight connections between the U.S. and Chinese economies, China's continued prosperity—and its energy security—will matter to the United States.

From this perspective, the United States is more likely to put greater pressure on other leading powers to "burden-share" in the Middle East rather than disengage from the region. Over time, Washington may direct this argument not only at its allies—particularly in Europe—but also at Beijing, which has been seen as "freeloading." The latter simultaneously benefits from extensive and expensive U.S. security efforts in the Middle East, avoiding this responsibility itself, and complains from the sidelines when it appears politically advantageous to do so.

It is worth recalling that Beijing's focus on territorial disputes in the South China Sea and the East China Sea likely derives from two energy-related issues: China's direct interest in resource development in the contested areas (now apparent in the South China Sea) and its broader desire for secure sea lanes for energy imports (and manufacturing exports) on which China depends for continued economic growth. Since China's leaders depend on rapid job creation to avoid widespread social discontent and potential political instability, the disputes may look much more significant from Beijing than they sometimes do elsewhere.

---

[25]Japan Country Brief, Energy Information Administration,www.eia.gov/countries/ cab.cfm?fips=JA (last accessed: July 1st, 2014).

[26]China Country Brief, U.S. Energy Information Administration, Revised April 22, 2013, www.eia.gov/countries/cab.cfm?fips=CH (last accessed: July 1st, 2014).

When considering the Europe-Middle East-Asia triad it is imperative to take into account the perspective of governments in the Middle East. While Americans and others wonder about Washington's plans in the region, it is perhaps less interesting to ask whether America will "leave" the Middle East than whether the Middle East might "leave" the United States. Few have investigated in any detail how major energy exporters in the region might react if the United States indeed becomes a progressively less important customer.

Washington originally developed close partnerships with Saudi Arabia and other major energy exporters in no small part because America and American companies were top buyers. If the United States sharply reduces its economic ties to the Persian Gulf exporters, American leaders may find some governments to be less interested in the United States and its goals and preferences—especially its ideas about their governance and their regional policies. The key question, therefore, is to what extent do America's relationships with Middle East energy exporters depend on economics alone as distinct from security cooperation and other shared interests. Ongoing negotiations with Iran over its nuclear program have already exposed significant differences between the United States and Saudi Arabia, as has the civil war in Syria. Ironically, American energy self-sufficiency could actually reduce U.S. involvement and influence in the Middle East without any particular decision by the U.S. government.

In this context, a related question is how China's growing energy imports from the Middle East could affect U.S. ties to leading oil exporters there. China has been actively cultivating relations with energy-rich governments in the Middle East, Central Asia, and Africa—including longtime U.S. partner, Saudi Arabia. In 2006, incoming King Abdullah visited Beijing, becoming the first Saudi King to do so since the two countries established diplomatic relations in 1990. China's oil imports from Saudi Arabia have roughly doubled since King Abdullah's trip, and at a little over 1 million barrels per day now account for about one-fifth of its overall oil imports.[27] Impor-

---

[27]The U.S. Energy Information Administration's Country Brief for China, updated September 4, 2012, sets China's 2011 imports from Saudi Arabia at 1.005 million barrels per day. In 2005, China's imports from Saudi Arabia were 500,000 barrels per day, according to Mahmoud Ghafouri, "China's Policy in the Persian Gulf," www.mepc.org/journal/middle-east-policy-archives/chinas-policy-persian-gulf?print (last accessed: July 1st, 2014).

tantly, however, Beijing has demonstrated little interest in a meaningful security role in the Middle East, preferring to benefit from U.S. and European efforts.

Nuclear Energy, Coal and Renewables

The last decade has been tumultuous for the nuclear energy sector. As oil and natural gas prices rose internationally in the early twenty-first century—and competition among consumers escalated—many governments became increasingly interested in nuclear power as a means to ensure reliable domestic energy supplies at what then appeared likely to be reasonable prices relative to other options. Nuclear energy was also attractive in comparison to coal due to its dramatically lower greenhouse gas emissions. At the same time, some governments may well have seen an indigenous nuclear power program as a prudent but internationally-acceptable step toward nuclear weapons capability.

Since that time, however, governments and publics in a number of developed democracies have become increasingly skeptical of nuclear power on environmental and safety grounds even as economic trends have undermined its competitiveness. Japan's abrupt nationwide nuclear shutdown after the 2011 Fukushima accident and Germany's subsequent decision to phase out nuclear energy by 2022 have been the most visible steps away from nuclear energy, though Tokyo has begun the slow and uncertain process of restarting reactors. Following the Fukushima nuclear accident, however, even France is considering scaling back its reliance on nuclear energy from approximately 75% to 50% of electricity generation.[28]

These decisions must be understood within the context of domestic politics in each country—in each case, the political left played a decisive role. The Fukushima accident occurred during the tenure of former Japanese Prime Minister, Naoto Kan of Democratic Party of Japan—a heterogeneous coalition including Japan's former socialist party, and Kan responded to the crisis by pledging to abandon nuclear

---

[28]"France's PM Says Bill On Closing Fessenheim Nuclear Plant to be Presented This Fall," Geraldine Amiel, *Wall Street Journal*, http://online.wsj.com/article/BT-CO-20130530-708771.html?mod=googlenews_wsj (last accessed: July 1st, 2014).

power—a policy since partially reversed by current Prime Minister Shinzo Abe and his Liberal Democratic Party. France's new approach is a high-profile initiative of the country's new Socialist President, Francois Hollande. In Germany, the decision by conservative Chancellor, Angela Merkel, was driven in no small part by electoral politics—and the German left appears set to play a greater political role after the country's fall 2013 elections.

In the United States, the Bush Administration pressed for a "nuclear renaissance" that has not happened, due primarily to America's changing energy economics but also to weaker action by the Obama Administration, ongoing regulatory obstacles, and continued public concerns. In America, construction of new reactors has stalled and the closure of a California nuclear plant has emboldened anti-nuclear activists.

At the same time, however, soaring electricity demand in developing nations appears to be driving an expansion of nuclear generating capacity in China and elsewhere. According to the International Atomic Energy Agency, China currently has 16 nuclear reactors in operation, 26 under construction, and 42 planned. Moreover, also according to the IAEA, 36 of 65 nuclear reactors under construction globally are being built in Russia and China and a further nine are in India and Pakistan. Seventy-seven of 114 planned reactors are also to be in Russia and China—and the prospects for 20 planned reactors in the United States and 10 in Japan seem uncertain. Nuclear power generation may be moving from developed democracies to China, Russia and the developing world.

Of course, even if China builds all of the planned facilities, it will have fewer reactors than the 104 now operating in the United States. There is little reason to expect that America will shut down a significant number of nuclear reactors prematurely. Moreover, the United States, its European allies, Japan and South Korea operate about three-quarters of the world's 435 reactors today—so a fundamental change in the global distribution of nuclear power plants would likely take decades if it happens at all. That said, the global distribution of nuclear construction has already changed and could have important implications that few have yet examined in depth.

The slow death of nuclear power in the West and Japan could have a profound impact on technological leadership, competitiveness, and security. With not only new reactors but even replacements taken off the table in some developed democracies—and a lack of fair and open competition in many other markets—Western firms might face growing difficulties sustaining competitive manufacturing capabilities, human capital, and technological innovation over time. Political restrictions on nuclear technology sales to developing countries could contribute to this problem to varying degrees as well by limiting where companies can compete. New French-Japanese efforts at nuclear energy cooperation appear in part to be a response to these pressures.

Moreover, if Japanese and Western suppliers lose market share, their governments may also lose international influence on non-proliferation issues. Notwithstanding the formal rules of the global non-proliferation regime, the greatest practical leverage historically may well have derived from a dominant position in the marketplace—a critical form of Soft Power. This could considerably complicate efforts to prevent particular governments from obtaining nuclear energy technologies that inherently convey nuclear weapons capabilities.

More immediately, the shift away from nuclear power is having real consequences for many nations. Germany's decision to shut down its nuclear power plants has led to increased coal consumption that undermines its climate policy goals. Japan has already faced dramatically higher costs for energy that create a drag on its struggling economy.

Broadly speaking, however, nuclear energy has been slowly losing its utility as an instrument of Western governments' national power in parallel with its global expansion. Nuclear energy is still a very important factor in energy security, in that it reduces vulnerability to market uncertainties and to attempts by others to employ oil or natural gas supplies to apply pressure. Considering traditional definitions of power as the ability to persuade others to take steps they would not otherwise take, however, nuclear energy offers fewer visible opportunities for leverage than the oil and gas that many countries need in large amounts on an ongoing basis. From this perspective, nuclear energy's principal value historically has been as an incentive for cooperation when the U.S. has offered to share nuclear technologies with key partners. Today, many others can offer this assistance if Washington is unwilling to do so.

In theory, America's considerable coal reserves could offer leverage similar to that enjoyed by major oil and gas exporters. In practice, however, coal is a bulky commodity relative to its price, meaning that trans-oceanic transportation can often become disproportionately expensive. This is reflected in the fact that only 14.5% of coal consumption globally was imported, compared to 27.2% of oil and other petroleum products and 31.5% of natural gas.[29] Moreover, in recent history coal markets have not experienced the long-term perceptions of scarcity that have fundamentally shaped contemporary attitudes toward oil and gas—an important psychological component of their unique place in the global competition for resources today.

Renewable energy is likewise limited in its utility as an instrument of power. First and foremost, wind, solar and geo-thermal energy are location-dependent; the United States cannot export sunlight, steady breezes, or underground heat. Countries can export electricity, of course, and many do—but generally to their immediate neighbors or others nearby since transmission lines lose significant efficiency over long distances. Given its location—and its two friendly contiguous neighbors—America has few opportunities to employ electricity (whether from renewable sources or otherwise) to persuade others to change their behavior. Other forms of renewable energy such as bio-fuels are simply not available in sufficient quantities to serve as an instrument of coercion or persuasion.

Still, renewable energy can and does contribute to America's soft power through its economic impacts, and through innovation and technological leadership. From a strictly economic perspective, the renewable energy sector is much smaller than the oil and gas sector, but roughly comparable to nuclear energy. Renewable energy production employs approximately 140,000 Americans, according to a 2011 study.[30]

---

[29]Calculations by the authors based on 2010 and 2011 statistics available at www.eia.gov (last accessed: July 1st, 2014).

[30]*Sizing the Clean Economy: A National and Regional Jobs Assessment*, Mark Muro, Jonathan Rothwell, and Devashree Saha, with Battelle Technology Partnership Practice, Brookings Institution, 2011, p. 20. The authors estimate the overall "clean economy" at 2.7 million jobs, but most are in areas like conservation, energy efficiency products and services, and waste management as opposed to the narrow area of renewable energy production.

Renewable energy can also contribute to America's international leadership in addressing common problems, such as climate change. The climate challenge and other global energy concerns such as access and affordability are generally not areas in which traditional notions of power apply—it is impractical to attempt to compel global reductions in greenhouse gas emissions or to force greater energy efficiency or access. But U.S. success in renewable energy, whether alone or in partnership with others, can increase global capacity to manage difficult problems in a way that strengthens Washington's global role, increases its influence, and improves its image.

Unfortunately, the United States has achieved only mixed results in this area. By emphasizing subsidies for technologies that are not otherwise economically viable, like solar power, the United States has diverted resources away from research and development of new technologies that could prove much more promising in the long term. The remarkable impact of shale gas on U.S. greenhouse gas emissions—by some estimates it has reduced annual CO_2 emissions by 400 million metric tons, double what the EU has done to comply with the Kyoto Protocol[31]—illustrates starkly how impressive results can come from unexpected places. Efforts to pursue a broad range of new technologies across many areas seem more likely to produce necessary breakthroughs than government-directed attempts to promote particular approaches.

Energy as an Instrument of Power

Energy contributes importantly to American power and appears likely to make an even greater contribution in the future. First and most important are energy's direct economic impacts, including its contribution to U.S. gross domestic product, job creation, trade and growth. For the U.S. federal government, which depends on tax revenues to "provide for the common defense," a bigger economy is clearly better and a long-term slow economy could be dangerous. As former U.S. Secretary of Defense Robert Gates has said, "fiscal insol-

---

[31]ILAR Working Paper #7, "The Gas Promise," Laboratory on International Law and Regulation, http://irps.ucsd.edu/dgvictor/ILAR_Working_Paper_7_2013.pdf (last accessed: July 1st, 2014).

vency at home will turn into strategic insolvency abroad that is more painful and potentially more risky in terms of national security."[32] Admiral Michael Mullen, former Chairman of the Joint Chiefs of Staff, has similarly stated that "the resources our military uses are directly related to the health of our economy."[33] From this perspective, shale gas and tight oil development are contributing not only to the American economy but to U.S. power.

Energy's role in the economy can add not only to the U.S. capacity to develop military power, but to America's soft power as well. As the U.S. economy grows, American officials have a more influential voice in global economic, financial and trade talks. At the same time, U.S. companies can win stronger positions in the marketplace. Similarly, new energy technologies are already attracting additional investment in the United States, both directly in energy companies, and in an economy where energy costs for many manufacturers are decreasing. This also enhances America's global role.

One of the most important ways in which energy contributes to American power may be the least tangible—the U.S. image both domestically and in international affairs. Since the 2008 financial crisis, economic uncertainty has contributed to domestic anxiety about China's rise and America's decline. This was evident in the quantity and tone of television advertising during the 2012 election campaign, both among presidential candidates and in Congressional races. Internationally, this same sense of American decline has been apparent in statements by foreign officials and especially in analysis and commentary in foreign media. Many believe it has contributed to China's international assertiveness.

In reality, however, China's economy remains less than half the size of the U.S. economy at market exchange rates, though it is rapidly approaching and may soon exceed the size of America's economy in purchasing power parity terms according to some estimates. With this in mind, China's high-single digit growth rates get the attention they

---

[32]Kari Hawkins, "Gates: Military Cuts Will Threaten National Security," www.army.mil/article/89291/Gates_Military_cuts_will_threaten_national_security/ (last accessed: July 1st, 2014).
[33]Ed O'Keefe, "Mullen: Despite Deal, Debt Still Poses the Biggest Threat to National Security," *Washington Post*, August 2, 2011, www.washingtonpost.com/blogs/checkpoint-washington/post/mullen-security/2011/08/02/gIQAhSr2oI_blog.html (last accessed: July 1st, 2014)..

do largely because American growth has itself slowed. This feeds worries about China's aims and about relative levels of defense spending by Washington and Beijing. Conversely, if U.S. growth returned to the levels of much of the 1980s and 1990s, China's economic advances would likely appear less troubling as the theoretical convergence point of the two economies receded into the future. Higher U.S. growth could also change how some Americans interpret Beijing's foreign policy behavior or cause some in China to re-evaluate their perceptions of the United States, which could affect the Chinese government's decisions. Of course, China also faces major structural economic challenges that some predict will slow its growth.

From this perspective, America's innovation-driven energy revolution—and the country's possible emergence as the world's largest oil and gas producer within the next decade or less—may be especially significant in that it clearly contradicts the narrative of a United States in decline. America's energy revolution is a clear example of how and why the United States has become an international leader and how it can remain one.

Despite the many ways in which energy contributes to American power, employing energy as an operational instrument of power is far from simple. There are many reasons for this.

The first set of challenges lies in energy's role in the United States and in the international system. Energy is connected to everything, including not only abstract concepts like security and prosperity, but also the very concrete realities of daily life. As a result, at the national level energy policy touches ordinary citizens in countless ways, starting with household budgets and extending to comfort inside homes, schools and workplaces, transportation and communication between them, and the environment surrounding them. These impacts on daily life make energy policy an inherently and intensely political undertaking. Thus energy power is not always easy to use.

At the national and international levels, the complexity and interconnectedness of modern life multiplies the (intended or unintended) consequences of changes in policy, establishing a high standard for prudence in decision-making. Few would welcome attempts to use leverage that backfires, as both OPEC's 1973 embargo and Russia's more recent gas and oil shutoffs arguably have in some respects by stimulating their targets to reorient their energy policies to reduce dependence on key suppliers.

A second set of challenges relates specifically to the United States. America's political and economic systems impose real constraints on its use of energy as an instrument of power, whether smartly or otherwise. Washington cannot order American energy companies to make particular investments or to subsidize other enterprises or activities domestically or internationally. The U.S. government can prevent or stop private commercial transactions only through legislation or other actions subject to the checks and balances of its divided government as well as media and public scrutiny.

Likewise, there is a clear philosophical tension between efforts to employ energy as an instrument of power, on one hand, and America's long-standing public commitment to free markets, on the other. This tension has not prevented Washington from exploiting other forms of economic leverage in the past and is unlikely to prevent America's use of energy-related leverage in the future; yet, it is an important consideration. Using energy as a foreign policy tool can impose reputational costs on the United States, for example, and could thus undermine U.S. efforts to achieve other goals.

America can minimize these costs only by using its "energy power" in ways that most others view as legitimate. This means using energy leverage to advance widely-shared goals and in a manner that appears consistent with stated U.S. principles. For example, U.S. leadership in imposing energy-related sanctions on Iran appears to have won acceptance if not support with the goal of bringing Iranian leaders to the negotiating table. If Washington's goal were to overthrow the Iranian government, the international reaction would likely have been quite different.

Energy and Foreign Policy

The U.S. government has clearly shifted its approach to international energy issues. The new Bureau of Energy Resources under the Under Secretary of State for Economic Growth, Energy and Environment is among the more visible bureaucratic manifestations of the change. Although the bureau is primarily a product of organizational consolidation, the decision to upgrade the offices handling international energy policy by placing them under a new Assistant Secretary demonstrates new priority for energy issues. Among economic sectors, only energy is separately addressed at this level. The decision thus creates a stronger internal advocate for energy-related considerations within the wider framework of U.S. foreign policy.

In assessing the relationship between energy and foreign policy, two broad categories deserve attention. First is international energy policy—in other words, U.S. policy on energy issues within the international context. Here, Washington uses a broad range of tools to achieve its global energy objectives. The second is instrumental energy policy—U.S. use of energy tools to accomplish wider goals. Though related, these two categories are analytically and operationally quite different.

The strategic goal of America's international energy policy has been to assure reliable and affordable supplies of energy in global markets. This derives from the recognition that U.S. energy markets cannot be fully separated from global markets and that international stability is a prerequisite for American prosperity. Notwithstanding rising domestic natural gas and oil production, this calculation appears unlikely to change.

In approaching these broad goals, the U.S. is likely to continue to use a wide range of tools and to work closely with its allies in Europe and Asia as well as other major energy consumers. This will surely include further cooperation in multilateral fora like the International Energy Agency (IEA) as well as in narrower efforts, such as multilateral research and development partnerships focused on new energy technologies. Success in developing and deploying clean coal, safe and proliferation-resistant nuclear reactors, fuel cells, or other new approaches could make an important difference in not only energy security, but other areas as well. Promoting innovation and sustaining U.S. and European technological leadership also boost their competitiveness with respect to other major economies.

One important objective for the United States and the EU should be to deepen cooperation between the IEA and China. While Chinese membership in the IEA seems a long way off—it would require Beijing to meet the standards necessary to join the Organization for Economic Cooperation and Development, the principal grouping of the world's developed democracies—greater information-sharing and policy coordination could strengthen the hand of major energy consumers in dealing with producers and exporters. Even if the U.S. becomes a net exporter of natural gas and oil, the size and diversification of its economy is likely to align its interests with energy consumers (who tend to favor lower prices and competitive markets) rather than producers.

Similarly, major consumers like the United States, the EU and China would benefit from greater security and stability in the Middle East, where long-standing conflict and uncertainty has been compounded by the political turmoil of the "Arab Spring". With this in mind, a cooperative effort to build a regional security framework could contribute to security and prosperity in the region while also reducing volatility in global energy markets. Negotiations to establish such a framework would not be easy—the role of countries like Israel and Iran in the talks and in any eventual agreement would be deeply polarizing. Nevertheless, if the United States and the Soviet Union were able to establish the Organization for Security and Cooperation in Europe during the Cold War, all parties should be able to find a way to create an analogous structure in the Middle East, particularly with the support of the world's leading powers. A structure like this could also provide new tools to address ongoing challenges.

Focusing strictly on North America, the controversial Keystone XL oil pipeline from Canada to the United States could further improve America's energy security, create jobs, and strengthen state economies along its route. Deeper U.S.-Mexico energy cooperation could also be quite valuable, though it remains a politically-sensitive issue within Mexico. One option to address some of Mexico's concerns might be to explore U.S.-EU engagement with Mexico on energy investment that would minimize fears of excessive U.S. involvement there.

Within the transatlantic relationship, the Transatlantic Trade and Investment Partnership (TTIP) could help to expand the U.S.-European energy relationship, particularly within the overall context of increasing U.S. fossil fuel production. In addition to its direct economic benefits, this could serve as an important new symbol of U.S.-European cooperation. America and the EU could also collaborate usefully to promote agreements on joint development of energy resources in contested regions, such as the Arctic and the South China Sea. If successful, this could mitigate sources of significant tension between major global powers, reducing the risk of conflict and stabilizing important regions.

Using energy as a foreign policy tool is quite different from using foreign policy tools to address energy challenges. How can the United States use energy as a policy instrument to achieve other goals? Notwithstanding new optimism about America's energy future, its system of government—and the politics of energy—will likely constrain such efforts, though it may be possible to use energy leverage to accomplish specific and limited goals.

One obvious step that the United States could take would be to liberalize natural gas exports to allow expedited review procedures for U.S. allies, including NATO countries and Japan. While the United States is unlikely to export considerable natural gas volumes any time soon, particularly when set against demand in Europe and Japan, such a step could provide some additional negotiating leverage to these key allies in dealing with their principal suppliers, especially Russia. Relatedly, efforts to facilitate investment could speed the development of shale gas and tight oil resources in Europe—at least in those nations interested in doing so—while also accelerating the transfer of key technologies and management know-how. Restrictions on U.S. crude oil exports also seem unnecessary in an era of expanding production.

As this idea illustrates, the greatest value of America's new-found energy power is likely to be in blunting others' leverage over Washington and its allies rather than seeking to compel foreign governments to action. Even setting aside the level of political consensus required to apply energy sanctions or similar pressure, America's enormous domestic appetite for energy is unlikely to allow the United States to become a major international energy supplier. U.S. exporters appear quite unlikely to amass the foreign energy dependencies beholden to some of the world's other top producers. The real impact of America as a net exporter of oil and gas lies in its wider consequences for international markets and the overall increase in available supply—something far from unimportant when remembering the scramble for global energy resources underway less than a decade ago.

With this in mind, opportunities for the United States and Europe to employ energy as a smart power tool are important but indirect. Energy, unfortunately, does not provide a "silver bullet" to address shared interests. Maximizing the smart power benefits of energy means increasing energy production—with an eye to its environmental consequences, and a balance between the two set by individual peoples and national governments—improving efficiency to limit consumption, and developing new technologies to help with each of these tasks. None of these goals is a new one, but the U.S. energy revolution can make all of them easier to achieve.

Chapter 6

Is it Smart Not to Be a Power?
The European Conundrum

Alain Lamassoure

Davos, February 1997, at the famed "World Economic Forum." I am invited as the spokesperson of the French government, representing Europe at a roundtable discussion with the provocative title: "Whose will be the 21ˢᵗ century?" Around 400 people are crowded into a packed room. The first speaker is Jeffrey Sachs, the American economist, very much in vogue because of the successful transition of the countries of the East, which he helped to instigate. His speech comes as no surprise: "Since the disappearance of the USSR and the collapse of Communism, there is only one superpower, the U.S., and only one universal economic system, liberalism, created, embodied and triumphant in America. The 21ˢᵗ century will obviously be America's century." This bold statement meets with some applause.

Asia is represented by the Indian Finance Minister. China has yet to make its entrance on the world stage. Not at all impressed, he retorts: "The South-East Asian 'tigers' have been competing to lead world growth for the past 10 years. Japan is the second economic power. The highest towers built by man are no longer the Twin Towers in Manhattan but the Petronas Towers in Kuala Lumpur. Asia also has unlimited resources, its population is 10 times that of the U.S. Asia will dominate the coming century." A large part of the room is in rapture.

The African spokesperson is a white colossus who is John Wayne's double, the South African Foreign Trade Minister still wreathed in the halo of the end of apartheid. He says coolly: "Africa is the world's youth. By the middle of the coming century, its population will be more than the combined population of China and India. The 21ˢᵗ century will be Africa's revenge on all those who have dominated it." These words are music to the ears of the few Africans in the room.

The Argentine Finance Minister then speaks for South America. He is succinct: "I agree with Jeffrey Sachs. The 21st century will be a great century for America. It is the South that holds the key to the future, however, and all of America will become Latin!" Thunderous applause.

As the last speaker, at the end of the table, I have listened to these pronouncements with growing consternation. What can I say on behalf of Europe? Suddenly, it comes to me. "During this and previous centuries, Europe has made many mistakes in the name of world domination. We have nevertheless tried to learn from those mistakes. We have ultimately devised a model of relations, which has reconciled our peoples to such an extent that war between us is now inconceivable. We are now prospering together at peace with ourselves and the rest of the world. If that is possible in Europe, it is possible everywhere else. The message that Europe therefore sends today is an inspiring message of hope: we can ensure that the 21st century no longer belongs to one of us, but to us all!"

I end with my throat tight with emotion, feeling very pleased with myself. Sadly, I am alone. The silence in the room is glacial. As soon as the round table comes to an end, the Indian grabs the microphone and yells: "I completely disagree with what the European has just said. Like all those before it, the 21st century will be a century of iron and fire and we will prevail over all decadent Westerners!" The rapturous crowd rises to its feet to applaud him.

At that moment, on that day, I understood that the world really was about to change.

Another World

Sixteen Years Later

An economic explosion. The first ten years of the 21st century have been the most prosperous in the whole history of humankind. The worst for Europe and the United States for 50 years. The best for all the other continents, including Africa. What is the pace of this change? It took Britain 150 years to double its per capita income; a century later, the United States managed to do so in 30 years; Asia now doubles its output every ten years.

A scientific and technological explosion. In just under twenty years, our daily life, the way in which we work, produce, create, learn and inform ourselves, our leisure and our dealings with those close to us have been turned on their head by innovations that we could not have imagined in our wildest dreams.

Among the thousand and one consequences of this genuine technical revolution, let us choose the spread of mobile telephones and internet access. Acts of mass violence in the thick of the bush are much more difficult when any bystander can directly broadcast images of them throughout the world. Similarly, the mass mobilization at lightning speed of participants in the Arab Spring would have been unthinkable without mobile telephones and social networks. Elsewhere, economic networking of the whole planet means that protectionism is no longer an option, and not just because every major national industry depends on its foreign outlets. Much more so because every sophisticated product includes components manufactured in the four corners of the world, wherever expertise and production costs are best. In the economic model applied so successfully by Steve Jobs, smart phones are designed and sold in the United States, but their touch screens are manufactured in Japan and their microprocessors in Korea, while the phones are assembled in China.

In addition to all these changes, there has been a population explosion. In primary school I learned that there were 2.5 billion human beings. My grandson is learning that there are now 7 billion, almost three times as many. His grandson will learn that there are 9 billion, at which order of magnitude the world population should level off and start to decrease.

These three explosions are extremely good news for humanity, opening the door as they do to development and modernization of all kinds. Taken together, their effect is the same: by reducing economic inequalities between countries and "technical" inequalities between individuals, they have an extraordinary equalizing effect. That is why demographics are becoming important again. Since the industrial revolution, two out of three people have lived in Asia, but Asia as a whole had remained on the sidelines of history. We wrote history without Asia.

Economic power has clearly, therefore, shifted to the global South. Since 2010, the old "Third World" produces more than Europe and North America, combined. Every year, South Korea files more European patents than France or the United Kingdom. South Korea has been chosen to build the UAE's nuclear power stations. In 2012, Samsung sold twice as many smart phones as Apple. The main customer of Airbus is not Air France or Lufthansa, but a Malay company, Air Asia, which has so far ordered 475 A320s. Airbus' second largest customer is a little-known Indonesian company, Lion Air, which bought 234 aircraft in one fell swoop. In 2012, Mexico again replaced China as the leading exporter of goods to the United States. Kenya, together with the diminutive Estonia, is the first country in the world to try out payment by mobile phone on a large scale.

In parallel with this economic wealth, military resources are also being stepped up. Every country that is gaining economic power, without exception, is also intending to strengthen its military might.

Another shift is less evident but just as important. In many fields, creativity, inventiveness, initiative, as well as the ability to harm, have gone over to the "other" side. There has been another potentially revolutionary change over the past ten years. The urban population has outstripped the rural population. The vast cities of the South are becoming colossal witches' cauldrons in which other unprecedented dimensions of the 21st century are brewing, whether in the areas of architecture, planning, social policy, ethnic and religious mix, the fight against crime, methods of mass education and slum management and the eradication of urban problems on an unimaginable scale.

We are aware of the shift in economic power. We are very concerned about the "relocation" of our industrial jobs and the arms race under way in Asia. We still have the impression, however, that although we do not lead world affairs, we still provide the benchmarks, the main policy orientations, the "agenda".

Peoples' aspirations for liberty, dignity and democracy seem to bear us out. These are universal values and we can take credit for trying them out a century before everyone else. They draw on our *example*, but owe nothing to our *influence*. Colonialism, neo-colonialism, as well as post-colonialism, are a thing of the past. As Westerners, however, we still continue to believe, on both sides of the Atlantic, that we are the only ones who can decide what is good and what is bad for the world. That time is over.

In 1994, agreement between the United States and the European Union made it possible to sign the world trade agreement that concluded the Uruguay Round. Ten years later, India and Brazil coolly stymied the Doha Round. Since then, international trade has been organized around a series of bilateral preferential trade agreements between the major regions.

In the environmental realm, Europeans, more so than Americans, have continued to spearhead reductions of greenhouse gas emissions. Without China and Brazil, however, the agreements, signed in Copenhagen and Rio, are meaningless: climate warming will not be a global priority. In Europe itself, the Germans have been the first to espouse this conclusion: the immediate shutdown of seven nuclear power stations, decided after the Fukushima disaster, has had to be offset by buying more Russian gas and, in the last few months, U.S. coal.

The Paradox of the West

History sometimes has a sense of humor. This major shift, to the detriment of the West, is nevertheless the result of the West's main achievement: peace.

The world has been at peace for close to seventy years. That might not be the view of the veterans of Korea, Vietnam, Afghanistan and Iraq or the wars of decolonization. No one can forget the horrendous images of September 11, and no year passes without new conflicts breaking out on several continents. Since 1945, however, the major powers have not gone to war. Although the Cold War complicated and slowed down relations of all kinds between the two halves of the world, the collapse of the Soviet bloc helped everywhere to free remarkable aspirations for development, for trade, for progress in all its forms. Globalization is the unplanned child of world peace.

No country has made more of a contribution to that world peace, following the two World Wars, than the U.S.: the staunch line taken by its leaders throughout the crises of the Cold War, the robustness of the Atlantic Alliance, the skillful way in which the White House reacted to the break-up and then the collapse of the Soviet Union testify to this. The United States is now the most surprised and the most discomfited by this new world order. When the Oslo Accords were being signed, Shimon Peres shrewdly said: "When a country loses its enemy, it loses its foreign policy." The sudden death of the Soviet Union did not just deprive Washington of its foreign policy. It opened the doors to a new world, offering new opportunities and posing new threats. There is no doubt, however, that we are playing a new game whose rules have yet to be devised. Once an enemy disappears, the first political reflex, as old as history itself, is to ask: who is next? For the first time in history, it is not entirely certain that there will be a next enemy. The nuclear deterrent is still in place—and is not the only deterrent. Day after day, throughout the world, the unhoped-for benefits of such a long peace are palpable. Billions of people have been saved from famine or rescued from poverty in the past twenty years. When peace makes it possible to escape from the curse of poverty, it is the best possible deterrent against war.

Does this mean that war is now a thing of the past? Are we finally stepping into an era in which war will be as exceptional as peace has been to date? Of course not. Nuclear proliferation rages uncontrolled, a dangerous arms race is under way between all the emerging countries, a growing number of States are gaining access to the most sophisticated military technologies, and globalization is giving terrorist groups the opportunity to wreak unprecedented harm, while in Africa the successive tragedies in the Great Lakes region show that the machete may also be a weapon of mass destruction. At global level, however, the main players are gambling on a sustainable peace. All of a sudden we are in a game whose rules we do not know.

The way in which the U.S., and Europe, have reacted to the post-Cold-War world shows that they have failed to understand that the rules have changed. The end of Communism has not been marked by the universal triumph of human rights, the rule of law, peaceful coexistence, tolerance and our modern concept of democracy: quite the reverse. The early years of the 21st century saw the Muslim world returning to a fundamentalism predating the scientific revolution. Similarly, military superiority, even when overwhelming, has proven to be not only powerless but also counter-productive in our attempts to convince even small nations of the benefits of our friendship. It is very revealing that the reasons given by the Americans for remaining in Afghanistan after the defeat of the Taliban, and then for invading Iraq, like those advanced by France for its intervention in Mali, are exactly the same as those put forward by the leaders of the colonizing countries at the end of the 19ᵗʰ century. The words may be different, but it is still a case of exporting our model and liberating people from the thrall of archaic dictatorships and fundamentalist religions so that they may escape from underdevelopment and gain access to universal values.

The Somali pirates are an even more interesting case. For seven years, a few thousand illiterate fishermen in their motor-driven longboats have been thumbing their noses at the largest international armada ever put together since the Second World War. Even as allies, U.S., European, Russian, Chinese, Indian and Korean naval forces are powerless because they do not feel that they have the right to fire. A few cannon shots would be enough. Even when hard power could be effective, however, it is impossible. The time has come for a change of paradigm.

The Rules of a World in Lasting Peace

The unprecedented situation in which we now find ourselves throughout the world has various features.

1. Peace which is lasting, but troubled and with no solid foundations. The main difference from all the previous periods, including the Cold War, is that an all-out war, involving two or more leading players, is now highly unlikely. Regional conflicts, potentially very bloody, between over-armed middle-ranking powers, continue nevertheless to be very likely, with a risk of contagion that is greatly increased by globalization. Any threat to energy supplies, staple foodstuffs or strategic metals would immediately extend the list of states tempted to intervene.

There is little doubt, moreover, that fresh civil wars will break out, and may be contagious. Such conflagrations are extremely difficult to predict and, by definition, extremely difficult for the international community to control. In Europe, we should remember the Calvary of Bosnia fifteen years ago. In Africa, we saw the carving up of the Congo, ten years ago, with the avid assistance of neighboring countries, at the cost of more than two million lives. As matters stand, the whole of the Sahel is being destabilized by the consequences of the civil war in Libya, just as the whole of the Middle East could be destabilized by poor international management of the war in Syria. What would happen tomorrow if the shift from Communist totalitarianism to democratic transition was not as peaceful in China as it was in the Soviet Union yesterday? Miracles only happen once. The West obviously has to take every step that it can to prevent and protect itself against, this type of conflict.

2. The world is no longer dominated by one power or group of powers. Several of the major powers are now players in the world game. That game will be permanently open to others. The major powers are becoming more and more interdependent. Information, knowledge, goods and élites have never circulated so rapidly, easily and completely between rival and potentially hostile countries.

3. The more the world is interdependent, the more everyone's progress has spin-off effects and the more contagious one-off crises become. Interdependency ratchets up what the economists call the "systemic" risk. The world therefore needs more rules and a system for preventing and dealing with all kinds of crises: health, environmental, economic, financial, political and so on.

In other words, "globalized" issues are increasing in number, especially as scientific and technical progress now means that mankind's action may be planetary in scale, for better or for worse. In his inaugural address in 1960, John F. Kennedy referred to the wonderful words of Samuel Pisar: "For man holds in his mortal hands the power to abolish all forms of human poverty and all forms of human life."[1] This was in the second half of the 20th century, with the prospect of unending growth and the threat of all-out nuclear war. Fifty years on, man also holds the power to modify biologically all forms of life, to degrade soil and subsoil irreversibly and to alter the climate of all or part of the planet. Moreover, man can invent materials, appliances and services which would have defied the imagination of science fiction writers half a century ago.

4. With no dominant power or undisputed world organization, these globalized issues are often orphans; nobody feels "responsible" for them. Even a list of these issues has yet to be drawn up. In other words, the

---

[1] See John F. Kennedy: "Inaugural Address," January 20, 1961. Online by Gerhard Peters and John T. Woolley, *The American Presidency Project.* http://www.presidency.ucsb.edu/ws/?pid=8032 (Accessed June 1st, 2014).

problems which are fundamental for our century, which are of concern to more or less the whole world, and which nobody is really tackling head on, require leadership.

5. *The smart networking of all the players concerned by global problems has to be part and parcel of the governance of this globalized century.* This includes states, existing or future international organizations, the scientific community, moral and religious authorities, NGOs and so on.

On such a chessboard, effective results will only be exceptionally achieved by pure force, by hard power, whether it is actually brought into play or merely brandished. Nor will soft power, implicitly acknowledged and accepted by others, be enough on its own. There will be a play of influence between rival and equal partners. What will be most important will be the ability to convince, win over and rally allies, to understand others and to seek out the common interest in order to implement a long-term strategy. All of this will have to be accomplished while grasping any unexpected opportunities, to try to make success collective in nature and to show that failure is down to all. In short, responsibility has to become infectious. Power will be exercised in a horizontal rather than a vertical way.

6. *Influence.* In this game, the West's chance lies in the fact that the principles on which the post-war order has been founded, and the organizations responsible for them, are not really contested by the emerging powers. Europe and the United States continue to have an influence in these organizations that goes beyond the power they currently wield, however, this situation will not last. Now we need to have clear ideas and draw up a collective strategy.

The Disappearing Continent

At the dawn of the 21st century, Europe has disappeared from the world political arena. The main reason for this is not that others have emerged. It is stranger than that. The Europeans have managed, on their own, to put themselves between the parentheses of history. They, like the Americans, are the victims of their greatest historical success: the reconciliation of European peoples. In the space of two generations, Europe has gone from a state of ongoing war between congenital enemies to a lasting peace between countries working within the same political Union. This miracle is the result of what we call the European integration. So far-reaching a reconciliation would never have been possible if, for decades, the political, administrative, economic, scientific and cultural elites, trade union organizations, local authorities, schools and charitable associations had not been involved in this extraordinary common project to build a political Union between sovereign states. The project's strength lies in its ability to overcome all obstacles, to advance towards and against everything. Its weakness is that it is slow-moving. It will take a century. That time scale, familiar to historians, is out of kilter with political time, punctuated as it is by the elections held every four or five years. Nobody yet knows how to make it compatible with *media time*, which requires a historic event every day.

The difficulty of European integration can be attributed to the resolve to reconcile overall unity with the sovereignty of the states that make up the Union. Uniform rules are needed in the European economic area and, in this century of giants, the twenty-eight Member States need to draw on the combined weight of their 500 million citizens to defend their common interests. At the same time, none of these twenty eight Member States is willing to give up its sovereignty within a federation along the lines of the United States: some, like France, Spain and the United Kingdom, because they are old countries; others, like the Baltic States, Slovenia and the Czech Republic, because they have only recently gained their independence.

In order to try to combine these two apparently conflicting demands—unity and diversity—the Europeans are constructing an elaborate political architecture, juxtaposing a federal and a confederal model.

The powers transferred to the Union are exercised using a federal model. European law requires agreement between a lower house representing the people, the European Parliament, and an upper house representing States, the Council of Ministers. The Member States have agreed to transfer a large part of their legislative power to the Union regarding economic, agricultural, industrial, monetary, financial, banking and environmental regulation, competition law, public procurement, the law on companies and persons in the European area, and minimum rules on labor law.

On the other hand, power over policies connected with national identity (education, culture) or involving solidarity within society (redistribution between the rich and the poor, health, pensions) continues to be largely national in nature. The result is that the Union is a legal giant and a budgetary dwarf. Lawyers estimate that around two thirds of the legal rules which now apply in Europe are drawn up at Union level, while the Union's budget is at present no more than 1% of overall GDP.

At the same time, their national interests are now so interdependent that the twenty-eight Member States have no choice but to coordinate their sovereign policies in the key areas of budgetary policy, foreign policy and defense. A confederal model is used for this coordination. It is put into practice by the Council of Ministers and the European Council—the summit at which Member State leaders meet.

Stepped up since the 2008 financial crisis, this coordination means that those involved are working together much more intensively: a finance minister meets his European counterparts more often than the other members of his or her own national government. Every government has to submit its draft annual budget for peer and Union review before presenting it to its national parliament. Decisions, however, are taken by consensus—as long as state respects the deficit and public debt safeguards (no more than 3% and 60% of GDP respectively), it has ultimate control over the content of its budgetary policy.

The complex nature of the machinery should not lead us to underestimate its results. Following the failure of Lehman Brothers, the Europeans reacted more swiftly and more effectively than the Americans. In the ensuing years, despite a long-winded and sometimes chaotic decision-making process, the euro zone withstood the worst possible storms. Every day for three years, the international financial press announced that it was about to collapse. Not only did that not happen, but the euro has continued to remain above the dollar value at which it was launched, and its share of world exchange reserves has even increased in recent months. Europe-bashing continues to be fashionable in U.S. politics but, at a time when the United States is being forced into budget sequestration, the Eurozone has halved its budget deficits and has a trade surplus of 200 billion dollars.

The limits of this method of governance are nevertheless a major handicap for Europe. Its first drawback is the slow way in which decisions are reached. In practice, the driving force provided in each country by what is known as the executive power belongs in the Union to the Summit of Heads of State and Government. Although they now speak on the phone or see each other several times a week, they are all taken up by their national responsibilities. The European Councils meet on average for two days every two months and can reach a common position only if there is consensus. In other words, they can tackle only one main issue at a time. For three quarters of the 2000s, the fine-tuning of what has become the Treaty of Lisbon occupied their agenda. Since late 2008, the repeated financial crises have eclipsed other priorities. This focus on their internal problems has meant that the Europeans have not really come to grips with the crazy speed at which the rest of the world is changing, or understand the new rules of the world game, or realize that their duty and their interest lay in playing a full part in that game.

The other drawback of this decision-making process is that it makes the various players less responsible.

In today's international scene, Europe can no longer be effective unless it is united. As matters stand, the Member States seem to be using their membership as a way of passing on their erstwhile responsibilities to the Union while taking no blame when it remains powerless. They are now so united that they no longer have any real national foreign policy, but they are not so united that they have any real common policy. Even in their traditional areas of influence, shaped by their colonial past, the United Kingdom, France, Spain and Portugal no longer feel able to take unilateral initiatives. They act within the international community, calling first on their European partners— and possibly NATO—or they do nothing. The Union's High Representative and the diplomatic network on which she can now call can intervene only when there is consensus between *the twenty-eight*. While this is more frequent than might be imagined, most cases involve minor crises or issues on which there is consensus among a large part of the international community, e.g., Darfur, the Iranian nuclear program, piracy off the Horn of Africa or in the Gulf of Guinea. In such cases, the Union's added value is technical rather than political in nature, making it easier to coordinate national diplomatic, civil, humanitarian and, in some cases, military resources, although that may bring with it the risk of tensions with NATO.

It might be thought that this no man's land of a union, which is too strong to allow for any individual initiative but too weak to allow for any collective decision, is fundamentally unstable and will have to progress, hopefully, toward real unity of action, or go back to full national autonomy. On the contrary, sadly, it is remarkably stable and is in the interest of every government. Every time a crisis crops up, those keen to act can demonstrate their resolve to their public opinion, and blame their partners' lack of understanding or the powerlessness of "Europe" when no one follows suit. Others can hide behind the lack of European consensus and do nothing. Or, more exactly, they can turn it to their benefit by planting their national flag on some superlative humanitarian action, gaining the maximum electoral advantage at home while running the minimum political risk.

In this gathering of 28 legally equal countries, not all obviously have the same weight. In practice, if Paris, London and Berlin are taking the same line on a major issue, the rest of Europe follows. Unlike the economy, where German successes are unabashed, in foreign policy the chink in Europe's armor is Germany. Seventy years after the fall of Nazism, Germany still does not feel at its core that it has any right to return as a major player in the international arena. Ninety percent of its external policy is taken up by European integration.

Outside Europe, its diplomacy backs up its trade and does so very effectively. The ghosts of the past continue to have a more or less paralyzing effect, however, when there is any question of taking part in military action, even if this involves no more than sending an observation plane. There has to be a debate and a vote in the Bundestag. It is impossible for Europe to play any real part in the Israeli-Palestinian peace process because no German government is yet able to give anything but unconditional support to the government in place in Jerusalem. At the time of the Libyan crisis, Germany's abstention in the UN Security Council from a resolution supported both by its European partners, the United States and the Arab League was the most spectacular demonstration of this national hang-up, which is hindering Europe as a whole.

Attitudes would change more swiftly in Germany if the "perpetual" peace that now holds sway in Europe had not underpinned the generalized pacifism that is part and parcel of public opinion throughout northern Europe. It is difficult to interest the countries of Eastern Europe in international problems other than their relations with Russia, the fate of Ukraine and the fate of the countries of the former Yugoslavia looking to join the Union. It is only really France and the United Kingdom whose history has given them an interest in the serious events that may occur overseas and the sense that it is their national duty to try to resolve them. Gaddafi's fall showed how effective—and how limited—their joint action could potentially be. Even when combined, their military resources no longer enable them to wage any "real" long-term war without U.S. surveillance and logistical support. Even in France, intervention in conflicts is supported by public opinion only if the number of losses on the home side is very small and only if enemy losses are not filmed by television.

Faced with the world's challenges, today's Europeans are afraid of being weak and afraid of being strong. They no longer feel they are in charge.

Only the Smart Guys are Powerful

Whether or not the Europeans are ready to rally together as a collective power is still uncertain, but if Europe becomes a power, it has to be a smart power—smart enough to turn itself into a power without worrying the Europeans themselves, to strengthen its architecture and decision-making process, and to pull together in this world that has suddenly become so alien to us.

Europe's chance is that the world needs it. The expertise that it has gained from organizing a multinational area remains unique. From Mercosur to the Association of South East Asian Nations, from the Southern African Development Community to the Andean Pact, from the African Union to the Asia-Pacific Economic Cooperation, there have been many attempts to use European integration as a model for forging harmonious economic relations between neighboring countries. Even when they are limited to trade, these groupings are still a good 30 years away from the degree of organization and the tangible results that the European Union has achieved. They have also had very little political impact.

The methods that have succeeded in Europe may succeed elsewhere and could be put to use throughout our planet. These are the triangular architecture of experts, governments and parliamentary representation; the method of the absolute deadline for achieving a goal which is ambitious but simple and comprehensible to all citizens; decision-making rules that are effective but allow everyone to feel at ease within the group; emulation by peer review or ownership by all of the collective result. These are just a few of the collective governance inventions that Europe can help to explain and disseminate throughout the world.

After twenty five years of customs union—the "Common Market"— the treaty known as the "Single Act" made it possible to place trade on a very different footing by introducing the same competition conditions for all in a common legal area. It also made it possible to improve collective efficiency by shifting away from the principle of decision-making by unanimity, to decision-making by qualified majority enhanced and improved by parliamentary vote. In that experience, what is there that could not be put to use in a transatlantic treaty that is not limited to trade in goods? Similarly, how can we adapt the decision-making system of organizations such as the WTO, paralyzed as matters stand by a mandatory consensus, which is now impossible and by the inevitable interdependence between trade rules and social and environmental rules?

If This Is to Happen, What Does Europe Need?

1. First, a legitimate leader. In the 21st century AD, just as in the 5th century BC, whether in monarchies or republics, whether in the northern or the southern hemisphere, at the time of the internet or before the invention of writing, there has been one unchanging constant in political life: hard, soft, smart or dumb, power is vested in one person. As the sign on Harry Truman's desk said, "the buck stops here."[2] The

---

[2]The sign "The Buck Stops Here" that was on President Truman's desk in his White House office was made in the Federal Reformatory at El Reno, Oklahoma. Fred A. Canfil, then United States Marshal for the Western District of Missouri and a friend of Mr. Truman, saw a similar sign while visiting the Reformatory and asked the Warden if a sign like it could be made for President Truman. The sign was made and mailed to the President on October 2, 1945. http://www.trumanlibrary.org/buckstop.htm (Accessed June 1st, 2014).

rule of democracy requires that the person is elected by citizens and is accountable to them. That is the European Union's main flaw.

That flaw was resolved on May 25, 2014. To date, the President of the Commission has been appointed as an international senior official, by agreement between the national leaders. The holder of the post was no match for national leaders fortified by the popular legitimacy gained in their respective countries. The Treaty of Lisbon ends this anomaly. José-Manuel Barroso's successor Jean-Claude Junker was elected by the European Parliament the day after its own election. He was elected by Europe's 500 million citizens. And for the first time the candidates from the European political parties campaigned in all 28 countries on a specifically European manifesto. These winners were elected on individual manifestos, are supported by a parliamentary majority and vested with a legitimacy at least on a par with—and numerically greater than—that of each of the members of the European Council. Europe now has a face, a leader, a "Mr." Europe. The broad guidelines and the main political choices will continue to be decided by the European Council, the agenda, the pace of work and the way in which that work is presented to public opinion and the outside world will depend first and foremost on that common authority. Around the Summit table, however, someone will take responsibility for pointing out that the common interest is not just the sum of participants' individual interests, and will have the legitimacy to make his or her voice heard.

2. Second, Europe needs to regain its driving force. Nothing succeeds like success. As long as it is the planet's sick continent, it will have no chance of attracting attention and interesting its neighbors.

Nationally, all the main European countries have to finish putting their public finances in order and reforming their welfare state and have to re-invent their own economic model. The 2008 financial crisis and its fallout showed that the three leading economies of the euro zone, Germany, France and Italy, lost the secret of growth. Despite its incredible export performance, Germany is finding it difficult to maintain a rate of more than 1% in the long term. The rosier performance of the United Kingdom, Ireland and the Mediterranean countries was built on sand. Once the financial and/or property bubble burst, they were in trouble. The treatment will be long and painful. It will not be made any easier by another silent ill that is eating away at Europe, just as it has done in Japan, i.e., the aging of the population with its direct effects on health and pension expenditure, and its indirect effects on the dynamism of our peoples. The necessary reforms are under way everywhere, however, and matters should improve in all those countries in 2015 and onwards.

The national economic policy coordination and peer review procedures stepped up two years ago should help the 28 national players to play in tune with one another. Common objectives that are easy to understand and measure also need to be added to the mix, e.g., returning to the top of the competitiveness rankings drawn up by the OECD, the World Economic Forum and other international organizations. The trade balance, the attractiveness of investment, patents, innovations, scientific publications, enterprise set-up rates, school and university results, etc., also need to be taken into account. Several Scandinavian countries are already in the world top ten of these major rankings. National self-interest continues to be the most powerful of incentives—and therein lies everyone's homework.

As a continent, Europe has to make better use of the political added value offered by the Union, with the new powers, institutions and procedures that it has been given by the very young Treaty of Lisbon. The Treaty came into force just under three years ago and has not yet been put to proper use. The financial crises following hotfoot upon one another meant that everyone's attention was elsewhere. It is, however, a very comprehensive toolbox for effectively dealing with those of our problems that can best be tackled in the territory of the Union as a whole. Some illustrations of this follow.

ENERGY. The Union now has the competence to draw up and implement a common energy policy. To date, it has merely provided a level playing field for the enterprises concerned and proposed ambitious energy saving and greenhouse gas emission reduction targets. In this very halfhearted framework, each country does as it pleases. The United Kingdom is resolutely reviving nuclear production, while Germany is trying to put an end to it. Poland is investing in shale gas, while France has gone as far as to ban any prospecting for it. All the Member States entered into a costly race to develop renewable energies in whatever way they could, before being forced savagely to cut the costly aids which made their profitability artificial. Biofuels were encouraged because of their ecological virtues, before being roundly criticized for their effects on the price of plants. European law may require level competition conditions, but nobody is really bothering to transport energy throughout the continent, to the extent that entire countries such as Italy, or outlying regions such as Brittany in France or Galicia in Spain, are threatened by a mass blackout whenever there is a peak in consumption in winter or in summer. Energy is nevertheless a crucial sector for industrial competitiveness, for strategic independence and for the protection of the environment. Only a European vision and a common strategy can make it possible to optimize national policies. Leaving everyone free to allow or ban certain types of energy, but rallying together to face up to external suppliers, harmonizing aids for clean energy, managing the coal market at the European level, and designing and financing energy transport networks. Moreover, European safety standards are the most rigorous in the world and could be offered as a benchmark for the world as a whole in the field of nuclear energy, and, in the future, shale gas.

IMMIGRATION. Some 1.5 million legal immigrants enter Europe every year to make up for the decline in its own population. In a context of massive and enduring unemployment, there is now precious little support for this immigration, brought about by the economic and political problems of the Union's African and Middle Eastern neighbors. It is the most politically sensitive issue everywhere in Europe. It is fuelling growing xenophobia and has led to the creation of new extremist political parties even in the countries of the north, renowned for their tradition of tolerance. Controls at the Union's internal borders were abolished as far back as 20 years ago, but it is only with the Treaty of Lisbon that the problem can now be addressed at the most relevant level, i.e., the European level. The Member States have to have the same rules on entry, movement, residence and working conditions for nationals of third countries. Customs services and border police have to be closely coordinated and, in the long run, merged under the authority of a European agency, which has already been set up under the name Frontex. The negotiations that each country now conducts bilaterally with migrants' countries of origin must be conducted for Europe as a whole by the European Commission. This will in all likelihood lead to a system of quotas based, for instance, on the Canadian system.

EXTERNAL ECONOMIC RELATIONS. With its annual revenue of 17.5 trillion dollars, more than the U.S. national revenue of 15 trillion dollars, the Union is now the world's leading market. It has a considerable negotiating advantage with respect to all of its trading partners. At a time when multilateralism is being superseded by the regionalization of international trade agreements, the Union has a strong hand. It is also the leading donor of development aid and at a time when the wind of freedom is starting to blow from North Africa to Burma, it has to take a far less timid line in ensuring the political conditionality of such aid. Similarly, as the euro has shown that it can withstand the worst of crises and has consolidated its position as the world's second currency, if the euro zone speaks with one voice in all the international financial arenas, it could have more of an influence on world accounting standards and revive the debate on ways of preventing wars between the leading currencies.

3. Third, Europe must also be able to mobilize the resources of hard power. Europe's main expertise is peace. It is not by chance that, in all the corners of the world in which conflicts break out, the first on the scene are often Europeans, e.g., the French *Médecins Sans Frontières*, diplomats attempting mediation, the officers of the Blue Berets sent for peacekeeping, and police, judges and tax collectors to help with state-building. That is why Europe's first duty is to disseminate this unique experience, to ensure that what is learned is channeled back to Europe itself—feedback as the military men would say—and that it is taken up by future generations. This goal has led to a plan to create a European Institute for Peace, a Swedish initiative on which the European Parliament is currently working with half a dozen governments.

However, the European Union cannot just be a large Switzerland. In a world in which the other players have not been inoculated against war like the Europeans, it would be crazy for them not to shoulder overall responsibility for their own defense. They will gain the respect of others only if they are able to use force when the need arises.

This common-sense view is widely shared by citizens themselves. In the continental part of the Union, 80% of the people questioned have for several years cited defense as one of the very first competences that now need to be exercised in common. Even in the United Kingdom, this is a widely-held view. As veterans of all the mediation and peacekeeping operations in the Balkans, Africa and Asia, the military officers themselves are the most convincing advocates of this cause. For twenty years, the Europe of Defense has been the subject of thousands of conferences, hundreds of speeches and dozens of initiatives such as the Franco-German brigade, multinational military staffs, the Satellite Centre, the European Air Transport Command, the Military Committee, the European Union Military Staff and battle groups. Sadly, this uncontrolled proliferation conceals the lack of any real political resolve. To date, cooperation in the defense industry has been really successful with the Airbus Group[3], BAE systems[4], Agusta-Westland and MBDA[5]; Europe has retained a sophisticated military industry. However, it no longer has the resources to buy its products for its own use. At the end of his mandate as Director-General of the Union Military Staff, Lieutenant General Ton Van Osch, declared: "I am standing down, but I feel bad about it. What am I leaving behind me? Armed forces, which are incapable of defending our common interest within NATO or within the EU."

The truth is that, more than twenty years after the end of the Cold War, the distribution of tasks between Europe and the U.S. to ensure the West's security needs a radical overhaul. In the current strategic context, NATO's survival is playing a part in making Americans, and Europeans, less responsible. NATO exists, and was strong enough to deter the USSR at the zenith of its power. It can certainly deal with any secondary threats in that area. Seen from Washington, what point would there be in overhauling a system that keeps almost all of the European allies industrially, militarily and diplomatically dependent on the United States? Seen from most of the European capitals, what

---

[3]The company was originally formed as the European Aeronautic Defence and Space Company (EADS) on July 10, 2000 by the merger of Aérospatiale-Matra, DaimlerChrysler Aerospace AG (DASA), and Construcciones Aeronáuticas SA (CASA). In January 2014, EADS was reorganized as Airbus Group combining the divisions for development and marketing of civil and military aircraft, as well as communications systems, missiles, space rockets, helicopters, satellites, and related systems.

[4]BAE Systems plc is a British multinational defense, security and aerospace company headquartered in London in the United Kingdom and with operations worldwide. It is among the world's largest defense contractors.

[5]MBDA is a missile developer and manufacturer with operations in France, Germany, Italy, Spain, the United Kingdom and the United States. It was formed by a merger of French Aérospatiale-Matra Missiles (of EADS, now Airbus Group), Italian Alenia Marconi Systems (of Finmeccanica) and British Matra BAe Dynamics (of BAE Systems) in December 2001.

point is there in worrying about our own defense? The old hereditary enemies are all reconciled within the EU, there is no longer any direct external military threat and, if the unforeseen does occur, NATO is there. In most European countries, an armed guard with a few proto-type aircraft and modern armored vehicles is enough to satisfy national pride. The will of the powerful NATO bureaucracy to survive even though the threat that created it has now disappeared is in effect encouraging political leaders to turn a blind eye.

There is no question as yet of putting together a European army. The system will long continue to be based around national armies proud of and fortified by their traditions. What we now need is to organize our armies in a complementary way and ensure that they are permanently able to act together under a common political authority. The Treaty of Lisbon offers all the necessary legal bases. It is only when it is sure that it can, when necessary, mobilize the weapons of hard power that the European Union will start to gain respect outside its borders.

4. Fourth, the time has come to draw up an agenda for the first half of the century. If it takes stock of globalized issues, discusses them amongst itself and then with its natural partners in NATO and the OECD, and then extends this forum to all the G20 powers, Europe can rediscover where its world responsibilities lie, and make sure that everyone else knows as well.

What Issues Do We Now Need to Tackle Together in the Planetary Village that the World of the 21ˢᵗ Century Has Become?

Strange though it may seem, the question has never been put in that way in the political bodies. Let us look at some of the collective threats and global commons exposed or created by globalization.

As has been borne out by recent events, it is space, with its massive near-earth meteorites, that poses the sole mortal threat to all forms of life on earth. This kind of threat could easily be detected and elimi-nated if there were to be sensible cooperation between the spatial powers. NASA and the European Union are both researching this issue, but separately.

The combination of the effects of proliferating contagion and the resistance of bacteria to antibiotics may pose a very serious threat to humanity as a whole. The H1N1 virus has been effectively contained. There is good detection of new resistant pathogens. The world, however, has yet to set up a proper organization that could enable such developments to be forestalled—through world regulation on antibiotic use, for instance. What would happen if a new virus with devastating effects were to cross the species barrier?

The international community has long been aware of the risks of nuclear proliferation. The basic treaty, the NPT, is reviewed and revised every five years. Events in Iran show, however, that its political base also needs to be revised. The West cannot really stand up to Iran because it lacks arguments. The authoritative argument, according to which only those who already had the bomb in 1968 are entitled to it, and not those who have managed to produce it behind closed doors since then, is obviously only going to impress those who currently possess such weapons. Focusing on the hate threats that the regime has made against its neighbors would backfire completely, as it would be tantamount to saying that an Iran governed by more moderate leaders would be entitled to such weapons, thereby undermining the whole foundation of the NPT. Europe has two nuclear powers, those being France and the United Kingdom. They could put their arsenals to political use by proposing an overhaul of the fight against the proliferation of weapons of mass destruction that takes account of the world as it is today.

The serious damage being wreaked on the environment on a planetary scale ranging from exhaustion of water and rare resources, mass disappearance of animal and plant species, pollutant emissions modifying the climate balance, and the destruction of unique areas or landscapes. This is one of the areas in which there have been the most initiatives and the Europeans have been most active, albeit with few results so far. They will have more influence once they have drawn up their own common policy.

The risks of disruption to the world economy. The lesson that has not been learned from the 2008 crisis is that financial proliferation is no less dangerous than nuclear proliferation. The money press is starting to run at full tilt again in New York, London and Tokyo. This is a field in which the European Union will soon be able to take a real lead. It has implemented the G20 goals in respect of the disciplines to be imposed on financial operators in an exemplary way and is in the process of completing its monetary union by a banking union, together with solidarity in guaranteeing savings.

The vast international traffic in arms, people and drugs has so far been dealt with only by partial or bilateral agreements. The same goes for cybercrime. Urgent steps need to be taken here as well, and Europe could again encourage its world partners to include these issues on a common agenda when it has tried out its own model within Europe, although much remains to be done.

If We Are to Tackle These Issues, What World Organization, What Framework, Do We Need?

Although U.S. Presidents have led the way here (League of Nations, UN, Bretton Woods bodies), the U.S. Senate's lack of enthusiasm has led the Europeans to take up the baton. They have played a key role in the creation of the WTO and the International Criminal Court. Generally speaking, as the world's foremost power, the U.S. finds it difficult to submit to the decisions of an international organization. Since the Korean War, its troops may well intervene on the basis of a UN mandate, but never under foreign command. The use that the countries of the Third World, sympathetic to the Socialist cause, made of the platforms of the UN or UNESCO during the Cold War is still fresh in the minds of Capitol Hill. In the 21st century, however, there is no longer a Socialist camp, no East, no North and no South—everyone is or aspires to be somewhat in the West.

International organizations have proliferated since 1945. As we have seen, however, some fundamental issues have yet to be tackled, and the new powers are not fairly represented in institutions such as the UN itself or its satellites. The democracies that we are should make us the first to call for a new balance, starting with the world institutions.

The UN Security Council has acquired a kind of world legitimacy. More exactly, all the States agree that, if there can be a legitimate authority, that authority is vested in it. How legitimate can a world council be when its composition continues to reflect the world as it was seventy years ago and has no seat for Japan, Germany, India or Brazil, and no representation of the thousand million Muslims. Forty years after decolonization, some countries sit on the Council because they were colonial powers at the time, and others are absent because they were colonized countries. We are well aware of all the political parameters for the reform of the UN: let us get on with it!

It was at the initiative of the European Union, led at that time by France, that the G20 summit met for the first time in Washington—at the worst moment of the financial crisis caused by the failure of Lehman Brothers. Aware that matters could not be more urgent, this meeting helped to restore confidence in all the world markets and stop any country from taking refuge in self-centered protectionism. Once the acute stage of the crisis had passed, however, G20's periodical meetings have become little more than routine, generating empty press releases. That is a mistake. Because of its composition, that body is best placed to adopt a world agenda that the other organizations can then implement.

Neither Americans nor Europeans, can allow themselves the luxury of turning a blind eye to a changing world. On both sides of the Atlantic, the parlous state of national budgets means that unprecedented cuts have to be made and, in a climate of ongoing peace, military expenditures are the first port of call for cuts, and are being slashed. But first and foremost, we do need to draw up an agenda for the next forty years. There lies the real question: what will be the situation in 2050? That still depends on us. Yet, for how much longer?

Chapter 7

A Smarter Power and the
Ability to Influence Behavior

Annemie Neyts-Uyttebroeck

European Security and Defense Policy: A Brief Sketch

The Amsterdam Treaty, which entered into effect in May 1999, introduced the concept of a European Security and Defense Policy, better known as ESDP, and incorporated the so-called Petersberg tasks. Those consist mainly of humanitarian and rescue tasks, peace-keeping tasks and tasks for combat forces in crisis management, including peacemaking. These developments were obviously related to the downfall of communism in Central and Eastern Europe and even more so to the tragedy that unfolded in former Yugoslavia, first in Slovenia and Croatia, and then during several years in Bosnia-Herze-govina. The total inability of the European Union to put a stop to the bloodshed painfully revealed an essential weakness, namely the absence of mechanisms that would have allowed the Union to use force in order to achieve its goals. This ability was introduced by the Amsterdam Treaty. It spelled out the tasks that could be performed under the ESDP, and created the function of High Representative for the Common Foreign and Security Policy.

In June 1999, Javier Solana, a former Spanish Foreign Minister and the former Secretary General of NATO, was appointed to that office, which he held until 2009. In 2000, The Political and Security Com-mittee, known by its French acronym COPS, was established to serve as a linchpin of the European Security and Defense Policy and the Common Foreign and Security Policy. Today, it is part of the external action architecture, though not of the External Action Service proper.

It is interesting to note that these developments were initially watched with some concern in NATO circles as the question arose how would the fairly new EU ambitions in the field of defense square with NATO's interests, not to mention with the interests of the

United States. This led to the 2003 so-called Berlin Plus agreement, which makes it possible for the EU to draw on NATO capabilities, although not unconditionally.

Soon after that, the EU undertook the first of its security missions, namely a police mission in Bosnia-Herzegovina. Over twenty more missions would follow, seven in Europe, ten in Africa and five in Asia. They are seldom purely military missions. Most of them are civilian in nature, mostly aimed at rebuilding local police, customs, and border patrolling or training the judiciary. Some are mixed operations. Even when they are civilian missions, they generally will comprise a military component, if only to ensure the security of staff and personnel.

In 2003, the European Council, the institution composed of the Heads of State and Government of the member states, adopted a document spelling out the European Security Strategy. A second such document was adopted in 2008. The 2003 document insists on the importance of prevention to counter threats to security, advocates a holistic approach to ensure global access to public goods, stresses the importance of multilateralism, and of acting in accordance with the decisions of the Security Council of the United Nations. The 2008 document is more pessimistic in tone, as it identifies a series of threats to human security. To name but a few: weapons of mass destruction, terrorism and organized crime, energy security and climate change. It sees building stability in Europe and its immediate vicinity as a major European responsibility and priority, and mentions both enlargement of the Union and its Neighborhood Policy as significant undertakings in this respect.

Still more important changes were brought about by the latest Treaty changes. The so-called Lisbon Treaty firstly unifies the decision-making procedures, even as it maintains unanimity for foreign affairs matters. The High Representative for Common Foreign and Security Policy is no longer attached to the Council, but is now a Vice-President of the Commission and chairs the meetings of the Foreign Affairs Council. She also heads the newly created European External Action Service, which is to develop into the diplomatic service of the European Union. In 2009, Baroness Catherine Ashton was appointed to this office. She is a former member of the British House of Lords. Her successor is former Italian Foreign Minister, Federica Mogherini.

Finally, the Lisbon Treaty introduced a new solidarity clause among member states, replacing the solidarity clause of the defunct WEU.[1] Thereby all member states are committed to come to each other's rescue in case of aggression, terrorist attack or natural disaster.

The European External Action Service, better known as EEAS, draws its staff from the secretariat of the Council, the Commission and the member states. It also has at its disposal a number of seconded staff members. At the Brussels headquarters, it has a Crisis Management and Planning Directorate, a Situation Centre, a Civilian Planning and Conduct Capability as well as Military staff.

This short and incomplete survey may be redundant for those who are very familiar with all the workings of the European Union, but it serves as a reminder that the Union, far from retreating from external action, is developing an active capacity and does so with the consent of the member states.

EU Foreign Policy: The Search for Smartness and Effectiveness

In EU circles the notion of smart power is seldom used, but I suspect that those same circles believe they are laying the foundations of a specific European approach to world affairs, which they consider to be smart. The Union prides itself on having developed a particular policy of mixing civilian and military elements in its missions and of putting human rights protection and rule of law at the heart of its actions. The Union, however, tends to overlook some important defects in its external action, notably overlooking the fact that it is seldom in a position to shape the order of things on the world stage.

The Union is of course a very peculiar political creature, consisting of 28 states that have pooled a significant amount of competences, thus creating a supplementary sovereignty, but nonetheless retaining a separate identity and sovereignty. Foreign policy, diplomacy and warfare are at the heart of statehood since time immemorial. It should not

---

[1] Western European Union or "Union de l'Europe occidentale." For more details see: http://www.weu.int/ (last accessed: June 1, 2014).

come as a surprise that sharing these functions with other states, let alone entrust them to other institutions, does not come easily.

This explains why the single most glaring defect of ESDP is the inability or unwillingness of member states to generate the necessary personnel, both military and civilian, to sufficiently man the missions the Union undertakes. The generation of sufficient troops for any given multilateral military undertaking is always difficult, be it in a NATO context, or in a UN context, or even within a so-called Coalition of the Willing. Things are no different within the EU. But there is progress. Even if there still does not exist much enthusiasm to pool resources, and do away with costly overlap, and even if the overhaul of military structures is slow, there are at present some 80,000 European troops deployed globally, under various banners. As the European Union is thus slowly developing a military capability and using it more often than ever before, the question about the aims and ends of these military undertakings becomes unavoidable. They should fit the European security strategy, that is, contribute to the fight against terrorism, international crime and secure energy resources. They should contribute also to the protection of those values, which are central to the Union itself, among which we find, first and foremost, the protection of human rights.

I believe most of the missions undertaken by the Union fit this bill, but how effective are they in the medium and long term and how sustainable would this policy be if it was to be pursued on a global scale?

How Effective is Military Action?

Before answering this question I want to comment on the role of military action in foreign policy or rather in world politics. Clausewitz famously said that war is the continuation of politics by other means. This implies that politics come first, and that war should be started only if politics fail to achieve their objective; that objective generally being a change in behavior of the other party or parties. The paradigm of war has changed since Clausewitz, but has it changed to the degree of reversing the priorities of war and politics respectively? Only an in-depth analysis could begin to answer this question, and I lack the space and ability to conduct such an inquiry, but I believe I may safely advance the idea that a change, which did occur undeniably, was a consequence of the 9/11 tragedy.

A "war on terror" was declared in response to the horrible destruction of the World Trade Center in New York, and has been pursued ever since. Whenever large-scale terrorism or large-scale criminal activities occur, military response seems increasingly to be the most forceful reaction. The situation in the Sahel and the anti-piracy campaign in the Indian Ocean are cases in point. Military action by itself does not entail a change in behavior by those who are subjected to it. Military action can put an end to bloodshed like it did in Bosnia-Herzegovina and Kosovo, end an unlawful occupation like the occupation of Kuwait by Iraq during the first Iraq war, restrict and prevent acts of piracy in the Indian Ocean or prevent massacres of civilians in Libya. Military action alone can achieve all the latter. What it cannot achieve on its own, however, is the installation or restoration of a functioning, democratic state, the rule of law and respect for human rights. That endeavor requires much more than military might, and takes a very long time to achieve, without guarantee of success. Bosnia-Herzegovina and Kosovo—two modest territories with small but heterogeneous populations of European extraction—are a case in point.

Military action, under NATO command and with strong American participation, put an end to terrible violence, which had cost tens of thousands of lives. Two decades later, in the case of Bosnia-Herzegovina, and almost one decade later in the case of Kosovo, democracy remains fragile, the rule of law is unevenly respected throughout the territory, corruption is widespread, and civil reconciliation is still elusive. These states have a tangible perspective of joining the European Union, to enjoy the free movement of goods, capital, services and most importantly, prosperity, peace and freedom to the more than 500 million EU citizens. Over twenty years of international efforts and ten years of European efforts respectively, tens of thousands of military and civilian personnel and billions of euros of support, have brought progress but have by no means fulfilled all of the original goals. The truth is that once a state breaks down or implodes, it is extremely difficult and time-consuming to reconstruct it, even in an environment and among people who have previous experience of a functioning state. When no such experience is available or where the memories have faded, such restoration seems even more difficult and time-consuming. Moreover, it must be done by the people themselves, in order to be sustainably successful. It is no wonder that military might by itself is unable to achieve such goals.

To return to the Sahel situation and the situation in the Horn of Africa, it is obvious that the break down of locally functioning structures has given bands of criminals and terrorists the opportunity to develop their activities, be they trafficking of human beings, drugs, weapons, or forcefully spreading extremely radical religious and political ambitions.

To prevent these developments, it would have been necessary to exercise pressure upon the various parties involved, find peaceful solutions to the conflicts between Mali and the Tuaregs, ensure better border surveillance along the extremely long Algerian borders, and to defuse and solve the Western Sahara situation. All of this should have been undertaken years ago, which would have required a level of international coordination and cooperation. In order to be successful, such efforts should also be sustained over long periods of time, no matter what happens in the meantime. The so-called Arab spring, which singularly complicated things even further, immediately comes to mind. Libya borders on the Sahel/Sahara belt, and what happens there (or not) inevitably has effects beyond its borders.

By evoking the fairly newly-minted concept of Responsibility to Protect, the UN Security Council authorized military action in Libya in order to prevent the massacre of civilians by Qaddifi. It did not include regime change in the mission statement. Qaddifi, however, was brought down, and the regime did change although it is far from clear in which direction it will develop. As a consequence of these developments, Russia and China who are permanent members of the UN Security Council, persistently refuse any form of military intervention in Syria where political protests against the regime, and the retaliatory response of the Syrian army are developing into an increasingly brutal and murderous civil war.

The calls for action to put a stop to the horror increase, however, and it might very well be that something will be undertaken in the not too distant future. Chances are that this something will be of the "too little, too late" kind as has often been the case with UN military missions. This is so because no government will readily put its own young people in harm's way in faraway lands to end a situation for which they bear no responsibility in the first place.

Further Considerations Regarding Smart Power

All of these examples serve to demonstrate that the exercise of smart power is far more difficult and complicated than one might think. Smart power is a clever concept that requires a high level of sophistication at all stages of its exercise.

To begin with, it requires clarity of mind and purpose. Where we stand and what we want to achieve are initial questions, which need to be answered before one can even start to pursue the exercise of smart power. Other questions may concern the kind of world we want to live in and, just as importantly, the kind of world we want our children and grandchildren to live in. From that angle, it seems to me that the answers to these questions simply cannot be limited to our narrow self-interest. Suppose that we want to live in a world that is safe and secure for as many people as possible, to begin with ourselves. Does this entail that we must prevent conflicts and put an end to crises all over the world because they might threaten our security and safety? Even if the answer were yes, there is at this moment no power in the world that could achieve this, even if it were willing to try.

Smart exercise of power must certainly aim at preventing conflicts as much as possible. This means that potential conflicts must be stopped in their tracks. It means also that conflict situations must be solved before they deteriorate into full-scale conflicts. This is not happening right now. Inside the European Union, the Cyprus issue remains unresolved. In the European neighborhood, several other conflicts remain frozen. In other words, they have been unresolved for a long time and will remain so, unless there is either an extraordinary pressure exercised on all parties, or a willingness to deal with the problem and solve it. Such frozen conflicts are most inconvenient for the people directly involved, but one should not neglect the fact that they could suddenly flare up and develop again into warlike situations.

Smart power requires much more resolve and single-mindedness than most people suspect. And it requires a lot of doggedness and patience. We do live, however, in an era of spectacle and show. It is an era of instantaneity and urgency, of brevity and apparent immediacy. An era in which foreign ministers and even the Pope tweet, is not very conducive to the patient, multilateral and protracted negotiations, which are generally necessary to defuse potentially dangerous situations, or to prevent fragile states from falling apart and imploding, thus becoming safe havens for terrorists and criminals.

The European Union, which entered late upon the political world stage, can benefit from this late entry and learn the lessons that should be drawn from the developments of the last few decades, which oversaw a multiplication of various multilateral missions under different banners, some successful, some much less so. In an increasingly interdependent world, smart power is more necessary than ever.

Part III

Powerful Assets for a Smarter Future

Chapter 8

Why Smart Power Needs to Get Smarter

Daniel Serwer

The Obama administration has repeatedly promised major reform and the strengthening of America's civilian foreign policy instruments as well as an improved interoperability in conjunction with its still powerful military forces. So far, little has been achieved. Washington, its friends and allies need to define better their future challenges and be prepared to reform radically their foreign policy institutions and modes of operation, especially in the Middle East and East Asia. The future demands less government programs and more private sector initiative, less military force and more civilian persuasion. Smart power is smart, but it is not easy. It will require leaving behind rigidities and legacies, and adopting unaccustomed agility and innovations.

In the United States, the requirements for civilian power were outlined in what I regard as the best document the State Department has published since the end of the Cold War: Hillary Clinton's Quadrennial Diplomacy and Development Review (QDDR), published in 2010.[1] It is a terrifically intelligent lay-out of the complex environment we face and the need to respond to it with all the many aspects of power, civilian as well as military. It argues for more coordinated and flexible responses to a wide array of contingencies in a highly uncertain world. It implicitly argues against a grand strategy, which would be inappropriate to the fluid and uncertain situation in which we find ourselves.

So how are we doing in implementing the QDDR? Can we mount the kind of civilian responses it calls for more quickly and more effectively than in the past? Can we coordinate the actions of our civilians and military? Can our governmental and nongovernmental organizations cooperate effectively?

---

[1]"Leading through Civilian Power: The First Quadrennial Diplomacy and Development Review" (United States Department of State, Washington, D.C., 2010).

The short answer is yes: there has been some progress. The long answer is no: the progress we have made is far from adequate to meet the requirement. If anything, we are falling further behind what is really needed, despite sometimes impressive efforts to keep up. We are aiming at a moving target, not a fixed one.

On the positive side of the ledger, the U.S. State Department now has a bureau dedicated to conflict and stabilization operations. It has been especially useful in Syria, where it has led the effort for assistance to the political opposition, and in Burma, where its demining efforts are helping ethnic minorities reach accommodations with military authorities who decided that they were at the end of their rope and needed to engineer a "democratic" transition before the state collapsed. We have also a much more amply staffed State Department with a lot of people who have served in Afghanistan and Iraq, working closely with American military forces. And we have a Defense Department that understands that it needs civilian help and has opened up a lot to receiving it, including by establishing its own Civilian Expeditionary Workforce.

But none of this is adequate. The QDDR may have been intellectually adept, but it was bureaucratically inept. The creation of the new bureau was not only a demotion in formal bureaucratic terms but also led to shrinkage in resources and dismantling of the Civilian Response Corps that was supposed to be a mainstay of American Smart Power. While the State Department can today hire people more rapidly to surge into a zone where people are needed, it has a limited standing corps of readily deployable people trained, equipped and practiced in cooperating closely with the U.S. military.

The practical effect is clear. If there were to be a political solution in Syria tomorrow, the State Department would be hard-pressed to produce quickly the people needed to deploy there. The Defense Department would likely be ready and able to deploy more civilians more quickly than State, because it does have a corps of employees prepared, trained and equipped. The only truly well prepared civilian agencies in the U.S. government would likely be Treasury and Justice, whose stables of economic and legal advisors are small but highly effective in helping stabilize macroeconomic environments and to begin legal reform in conflict situations. But that was also true 20 years ago.

USAID is not in much better shape. It has doubled and redoubled its efforts to operate in conflict environments more closely with the U.S. military. But no one would describe its cooperation with either State or Defense as seamless. AID continues to be dominated by a project-focused "development" mindset that limits its effectiveness in pursuing security sector reform, rule of law, property rights, public administration, and other priorities in difficult environments. In a world where weak, fragile and failing states pose many of our most severe national security problems, state-building is a central requirement of Smart Power. Yet, we are not much better at it than we were almost twenty years ago, when I arrived in Bosnia and tried to hitch a ride into town from the airport with the French troops.

Both State and AID have done a lot of running over the last two decades. But they have not kept up. Now they face a new problem: constrained resources. They have both done reasonably well over the past decade, though not nearly as well as the Defense Department, in capturing budgetary appropriations. But neither the situation in Congress nor the American economy will permit continuing growth. State, AID and Defense are all constrained by what we call "sequestration," which essentially is causing across-the-board cuts in agency budgets to levels not seen in years.

How should Smart Power react smartly to constrained resources? There are four answers: shift towards prevention, restructure, share burdens and enhance non-governmental efforts.

The needed shift towards prevention is something that should happen even if resources were not so severely constrained. If the post-war reconstruction of Afghanistan and Iraq has taught us anything, it is that building states during and after conflict is too difficult and expensive. The same can be said of the Arab uprisings: nothing about them suggests we know how to help revolutionaries re-establish a monopoly on the legitimate means of violence in Libya or accomplish a democratic transition in Egypt after the fall of an autocratic regime.

What we need to do is become much more anticipatory. This is not easy. Our governments do not like to hear that Mali might not have a strong enough state to combat Tuareg tribesmen returning from Gadhafi's Libya. In the fall of 1997, I asked my betters in the State Department to let me work on preventing war in Kosovo, where the Kosovo

Liberation Army was beginning to attack Serbian officials. No, they replied, you are a senior officer, so having you work on Kosovo would attract too much attention to the issue. Less than a year and a half later, the United States led NATO to war over Kosovo.

Our diplomatic establishments are not designed to be anticipatory. The State Department was founded in the 18th century. We think of America as a young country. But it is an old governing system, one of the oldest on earth. We have had only one republic. There are many more countries on earth today than when the State Department was founded, but the system of embassies and consulates we use today has not changed much in the past 90 years or so, since the professionaliza-tion of the U.S. Foreign Service. I first served in one of our embassies more than 35 years ago. There were about 800 people, American and Italian, in the U.S. diplomatic mission to the Quirinale at the time. There were still 800 when I became Deputy Chief of Mission there in the early 1990s. And there are still 800 now.

That is remarkable given the changes in the world over the past four decades: Europe's integration has meant many Italian sovereign functions have been delegated to Brussels. The end of the Cold War has made Europe a launching pad for NATO rather than the territory that needs its protection. Control of Middle East oil resources has shifted from companies to sovereign states and dependency on oil shipped through the Strait of Hormuz has increased. Asia has grown into an economic powerhouse.

The explanation for the size of our mission in Italy is legacy, and inertia. The legacy is from World War II. The inertia is not only in the State Department, whose diplomatic and consular functions account for no more than 10% of the 800 staff, but the dozens of other U.S. agencies with offices in Italy that receive services from the State Department. When I became Deputy Chief of Mission in Rome, we were fixing toilets for 400 American families. I got us out of that business, but my successors have gone back to doing it.

Some soft power advocates might see a big embassy of this sort with lots of mainly domestic civilian agencies represented as an advantage. It enables the United States to do some important things: Embassy Rome was vital to enabling our judiciary and police to help Italians break up the "pizza connection" drug ring and undermine the Sicilian mafia. So at least some of those 800 people are doing good things. You can imagine—and you would not be wrong—that I could give you some other excellent examples in the counter-terrorism business.

But even if I can be pleased when America uses "civilian power" to catch bad people who do terrible things, we do not need a big embassy to do that. To the contrary: that giant Palazzo Margherita compound on via Veneto is a target. Some of our other embassies are provocations, like the one in Baghdad. These are fabulously expensive operations sitting on high priced real estate that symbolize American power but do little to enhance or exercise it.

Modern technology has made our embassies antiquated. I can do good political reporting from a laptop in my apartment, as the International Crisis Group does. I can do good economic reporting from London with the occasional trip in country to visit local experts, as the Economist Intelligence Unit does. I can deliver diplomatic messages from my capital via fax, email and Twitter, as most governments on earth already do. Visits are easier, cheaper and safer than big fixed installations that are terrorist targets and prisons—even sometimes deathtraps—for our diplomats, who would much rather be pounding the pavement to get the real feel of the foreign capital to which they are assigned.

My proposal for restructuring the State Department and USAID would therefore start by shrinking our grotesquely bloated embassies down to 50 Americans or less, except in specific cases. Any agency not included in this ceiling by the ambassador would still operate under his authority but could be located outside the embassy in whatever premises the domestic agency chose. State Department would not provide services or security. Few domestic agencies would go for that deal.

The shrinkage of the American footprint abroad would provide very substantial savings in dollars and personnel. This could be used to create the kind of agile, anticipatory diplomatic corps required in today's world. Taking advantage of modern technology, these people would deploy to wherever they were needed to meet immediate needs, rather than worrying about legacy and creating the bureaucratic inertia that has saddled us with elephantine embassies and consulates in places where neither soft nor hard power is any longer of great importance.

This kind of restructuring of the State Department and USAID would also entail reductions in headquarters staff. It should be possible to produce several billion dollars and several thousand employees for an expeditionary corps of diplomats and civil servants who could project American civilian power rather than sit behind high walls in fortress embassies. This is especially important as we try to pivot to East Asia even while meeting unanticipated requirements in the Middle East. We do not have an embassy in Syria or Iran today, but we need dozens of diplomats working on Syria from Turkey (and I hope eventually from liberated areas inside Syria) and on Iran from Washington and Doha.

What is also important in meeting soft power requirements is greater sharing of burdens among likeminded countries. The UN, the European Union and the OSCE are already key partners for the Americans, along with a growing number of African countries willing to provide peacekeeping forces. I would like to see a much greater civilian capacity built up also within NATO. Europe resists that proposition, so as not to dilute EU efforts.

The Americans have been remarkably successful at burden sharing. Europe bore the lion's share of the military and civilian burdens in the Balkans interventions over the past 20 years. The first Gulf War was all but paid for, principally by Gulf States. Afghanistan and Iraq were U.S. initiatives, but there was substantial European participation in both efforts. Even the intervention in Libya, which began as a U.S. military operation, fell mainly to others as it ground forward.

What these burden sharing efforts need to be more effective is greater clarity and coherence about end-states, especially on the civilian side of the equation. What are we trying to achieve and who is in the lead? Initial cooperative efforts in Afghanistan faltered miserably because we could not answer these simple questions. Coherence was established earlier in Iraq, even if security circumstances conspired to make democratization there extraordinarily difficult. In Libya, civilian planning was left up to the Libyans and a small UN contingent, which we know now to have been inadequate. We should be planning now, jointly with the Syrian opposition, to answer end-state questions once Bashar al Assad falls.

There is one more thing we should be doing: nongovernmental efforts are clearly more efficient, more effective and more appropriate in many difficult situations today. They need to be increased. There are a lot of things that cannot be done by an official diplomatic mission. We have a number of good examples: National Endowment for Democracy, with its Republican and Democratic affiliates, the Soros organizations, the American Bar Association, or my alma mater United States Institute of Peace. But their resources are miniscule compared to the requirements, and they are increasingly under tight government tutelage. I would free them of that and give them consistent and increased resources.

This is the kind of smarter power I would like to see us acquire: it should focus on preventing conflict and instability, lead to a serious restructuring of our diplomatic establishments so that they become more expeditionary and anticipatory, share burdens within a clear concept of strategic goals, and shift resources to nongovernmental initiatives.

Kari Mottola, a retired Finnish foreign service officer and now professor, wrote recently about U.S. post-war reconstruction efforts, which are admittedly only one aspect of Smart Power: "Where America as a polity has come short is in failing to recognize, as a permanent national security interest, the need to design and pursue a *strategic policy* on stabilization and reconstruction. While the concept may be debatable and the capability may be constrained by developments, what those devoted to the cause call for is a policy with a sustainable balance between ends and means and commensurate to the responsibility of U.S. global leadership."[2] We are not there yet. Budget stringency and domestic political pressures require us not just to be smart. Smart power needs to get smarter.

---

[2]Kari Mottola, "Addressing a Recurrent, Variable and Complex Challenge: The Uncertain Trajectory of Stabilization and Reconstruction in U.S. Strategy Study," *Prism* 4, no. 3 (2013): 61.

References

"Leading through Civilian Power: The First Quadrennial Diplomacy and Development Review." United States Department of State, Washington, D.C., 2010.

Mottola, Kari. Addressing a Recurrent, Variable and Complex Challenge: The Uncertain Trajectory of Stabilization and Reconstruction in U.S. Strategy Study. *Prism* 4, no. 3 (2013): 61-71.

Chapter 9

The Transatlantic Trade and Investment Partnership: An Economic Agreement to Foster the Transatlantic Community

Tyson Barker

After years of economic unease and high structural unemployment, policy preferences of Europe's major powers begin to coalesce around a major strategic initiative meant to re-ignite economic growth and revive a key Western strategic project. France, under the leadership of a Socialist government after more than a decade of center-right stewardship, begrudgingly recognizes that policies meant to modernize its economy will depend on external pressure for reform. Germany and the United Kingdom, both governed by the center-right, champion the initiative. The UK, with its economy tilted towards services, assumes a leading role in pushing for liberalization. The German manufacturing juggernaut forces its neighbors to focus on ways of regaining competitiveness and sees the creation of a deeper common market as a means to do so. Beyond that, the leaders recognize the need for a new strategic logic to jumpstart a flagging community that has lost its moorings.

The year, of course, is 1986. The project was the Single European Act (SEA). The SEA revolutionized trade and investment flows across what became the European Union. It used the market to force member states to confront four key areas of economic reform: 1) liberalization and acceleration of product approval processes; 2) elimination of duplicative bureaucracy; 3) direct exposure to competition in product, labor and capital markets previously shielded by protective measures; and 4) socialization that will lead to more outward-looking, export-oriented companies. The SEA also had a deep strategic underpinning. It was the vehicle that revived the legitimacy of European integration by introducing a project that would enhance Europe's collective political and economic influence after years adrift. Moreover, the SEA became a tool for enhancing the push for structural reform across Western and Southern Europe to counter the emerging competitiveness gap with East Asia and, at the time, Central Europe. Since the SEA's implementation, the degree of cross-border trade intensity within the EU has increased dramatically.

Today, the Atlantic community faces a similar strategic and economic environment to that confronting the European community in the mid-1980s. Helmut Kohl, Margaret Thatcher and François Mitterrand have been succeeded by Angela Merkel, David Cameron and François Hollande, and today's Obama administration has a vastly different ideological outlook to Ronald Reagan's. The structural factors informing policymakers, however, offer striking parallels. It is in this environment that the negotiations for the Transatlantic Trade and Investment Partnership (TTIP), a comprehensive free-trade agreement between the United States and EU, were launched at the June 2013 G8 summit in Lough Erne, Northern Ireland.

In some ways, the push for the TTIP is essentially an attempt to Atlanticize the European single market. The aim is to create a robust commercial environment that encompasses almost all aspects of state regulation, from regulations dealing with safety, environmental impact and labor to sector-based regulation in industries from financial services to advanced IT manufacturing. In this, European and American negotiators would like to address the barriers of entry for market participation, which would increase commercial activity for large multinational firms and small- and medium-sized businesses on both sides of the Atlantic. At the same time, the TTIP serves to Atlanticize many of the same strategic goals of the SEA. It is an attempt in the wake of the post-2008 financial crisis to reassert the West's relevance as a hub of global economic activity.

This chapter aims to explore the principal macro-political motivations that drove U.S. and European policymakers to pursue TTIP, a project that proved elusive in the past, and some of the issues up for consideration if a politically sound agreement is to be reached. This chapter is meant neither to plot the contours of negotiations, nor to examine in detail any potential sector-specific reservations. Those issues have been addressed exhaustively in other works. Rather, this chapter examines TTIP's potential benefits through three lenses: the geopolitical, the economic and the distributive. It does so in four sections.

The first section analyzes how TTIP can be leveraged to affect changes in the international system consistent with Western preferences. For all of the declinism that has become a mainstay of the transatlantic relationship in recent years, it is important to recognize the immense coercive power that still rests in this relationship. That power and its ability to influence the normative behavior of people and states draw increasingly on economic rather than military weight. From Kiev to Bali, recent international behavior is replete with evidence of the power of the Western market to incentivize institutional and popular change. TTIP's potential to marshal this economic weight for political aims is a principal motivating factor for pursuit of an agreement, and negotiations have already begun to demonstrate this potency.

The second section examines what TTIP could mean for the American and European domestic economies in terms of welfare increases and job growth. The economic benefits for the transatlantic economic zone are significant. The Bertelsmann Foundation has conducted two independent studies examining these effects, each of which provides evidence that the tangible main-street dividends of trade liberalization between the U.S. and Europe are significant enough to warrant serious attention by policymakers. The first study, conducted jointly with the Atlantic Council, looks at the potential impact of a comprehensive TTIP on the U.S.. The second part outlines the findings of a Bertelsmann Stiftung-Ifo study on TTIP's estimated macroeconomic impact on the EU's 28 member states.

The third section looks at an emerging element of the TTIP debate—welfare-gain distribution. For the geopolitical and economic analysis outlined in the first two sections to be compelling, it must address how lawmakers can use policy tools to guarantee an equitable domestic distribution of TTIP's benefits.

The final section provides a brief consideration of the next-generation stumbling blocks that, combined with legacy sectoral concerns, could trip up negotiations. This consideration is by no means exhaustive. Rather than focus on the legacy sticking points that have stymied past economic convergence, this section provides three examples of post-crisis challenges that could prove problematic for negotiations.

The chapter concludes with an emphasis on holistic strategies that could provide the most effective avenue for TTIP's successful passage despite potential opposition.

TTIP'S Geopolitical Throw Weight

In the post-Cold War world, two big geopolitical ideas captured the imaginations of U.S. and European political leaders. The first was NATO and EU enlargement to include the post-communist countries of Central and Eastern Europe as a means of re-integrating these states into the broader community of liberal democracies. Enlargement was the leading priority in U.S. relations with Europe throughout the 1990s and was largely completed as a strategic project.

The second idea was the deepening of the transatlantic marketplace, the immensity of which has made it a cornerstone of the global economy. Together, the American and European economies comprise 50 percent of global gross domestic product (GDP) (41 percent in terms of purchasing power parity[1]), a size that provides a power base for continuing to set global economic rules. The totality of the U.S.-EU trade, investment and commercial relationship is almost $5 trillion.[2] If it were a country, this relationship would have the world's fourth-largest economy. The United States is the EU's largest repository for foreign direct investment, while the EU is the most attractive foreign recipient of American capital, attracting 50 percent of global U.S. foreign direct investment (FDI).[3]

The pursuit of a transatlantic marketplace has been almost Sisyphean in character. From 1990 to 2007, post-Cold War transatlantic economic relations were marked by failed-start attempts at forging some sort of arrangement.[4] Because tariffs are low and market

---

[1]Hamilton, D. & Quinlan, J.P. (2014). *The Transatlantic Economy 2014: Annual Survey of Jobs, Trade and Investment Between the United States and Europe*. p. 5. Washington, DC: Center for Transatlantic Relations.

[2]Ibid.

[3]Ahearn, R. (18 January, 2012). *US-EU Trade and Economic Realtions: Key Policy Issues for the 113th Congress* (Report). P.1.

[4]In 2006, German Chancellor Angela Merkel raised the possibility of a transatlantic free trade agreement in the wake of the collapse of the Doha Round. The effort eventually led to the formation of the Transatlantic Economic Council in 2007. See: Der Spiegel Blog (October 2, 2006). Trans-Atlantic Free Trade? Merkel for EU Agreement with US. *Der Spiegel*. Retrieved

access for everything from goods to capital is relatively robust, the greatest marginal benefits lay in greater regulatory convergence that can ease the standards and certification process for goods and open restricted areas in services. But this is not easy. Narrowly defined sectoral issues and deeply entrenched political interests around regulation derailed past efforts, and have the potential to limit a TTIP agreement to tariff reduction. Issues ranging from the approval process of genetically modified organisms (GMOs) to carve-outs for market access in audiovisual products and services have been perennial complications in the transatlantic economic relationship. These potential regulatory sticking points have been addressed exhaustively in literature on regulatory barriers to transatlantic trade.[5]

So why pursue a sweeping agreement now? For one, enlargement fatigue in the EU and NATO combined with the 2014 military withdrawal from Afghanistan risks leaving the transatlantic relationship without a strategic project that can serve as an organizing principle for the partnership, one that many observers lament has recently atrophied. The fiscal and budget debates in Washington and the eurozone crisis threaten to crowd out joint action in other areas. For Europe, the risk of a decade of introspection and insularity, including protracted negotiations of treaty adjustments, is another hindrance. Both sides are looking elsewhere and not at each other. The U.S. gazes increasingly to the East and the South, while the EU turns evermore inward. The specter of a centrifugal Atlantic is real.[6] Yet for Europe, TTIP negotiations would provide a direct transatlantic policy approach to the eurozone crisis, which continues to mar the continent. A trade agreement would also help legitimize UK membership in the

---

from: http://www.spiegel.de/international/trans-atlantic-free-trade-merkel-for-eu-agreement-with-us-a-440335.html (June1st, 2014).

[5]For a selection of literature on regulatory barriers to transatlantic trade, see: Bertelsmann Foundation. (2013). *Field Manual to Europe: Ten Memos for the New US Administration* (Report). Retrieved from: http://www.bfna.org/publication/field-manual-to-europe; Akhtar, S. & Jones, V. (July 23, 2013). *Proposed Transatlantic Trade and Investment Partnership (TTIP): In Brief.* (Report R43158). Congressional Research Service. Retrieved from: http://www.fas.org/sgp/crs/row/R43158.pdf; Lester, S. (July 11, 2013). Transatlantic Regulatory Barriers. *The Huffington Post*. Retrieved from: http://www.huffingtonpost.com/simon-lester/transatlantic-regulatory-trade-barriers_b_3580900.html (June 1st, 2014).

[6]A perception began to harden in European capitals that the U.S. interest in Europe as a partner was waning reinforced by the administration's decision to cancel the 2010 US-EU Summit, the first leaders gathering following the Lisbon Treaty's entrance into force.

EU by providing London with a leadership role that neatly reinforces its European and Atlanticist identities.

For the United States and the EU, whose relative economic might and concurrent ability can shape global economic governance, TTIP's motivations beyond the Atlantic are equally compelling. The international economic system is becoming increasingly Hobbesian. Global commons and economic rule setting are more contested. Institutions of global governance, such as the G20, the World Trade Organization (WTO), the International Monetary Fund (IMF), International Civil Aviation Organization (ICAO) and World Conference on International Telecommunications (WCIT), have each been stalemated in recent years.

The United States and Europe have to re-position their economies to engage more aptly in the coming rounds of international economic governance. Increasingly both sides recognize that their ability to set the global rules will diminish. The emergence of an order replete with spoilers but no coherent agenda-driver for the global economic system threatens instead. The fear is that the economic order will become ungovernable.

Forging global consensus is already increasingly difficult as many key middle- and low-income economies see their interests best represented in policies that favor technology transfer, more interventionist restrictions on market access, and the proliferation of state-owned enterprises. This puts such countries at odds with advanced industrial economies whose policies often place emphasis on intellectual property rights (IPR), openness to flows of goods and capital, and a deep ambivalence to government ownership of industry.

The recent National Intelligence Council (NIC) 2030 report, a consensus document of the U.S. intelligence community, identified the diffusion of power away from the West and the breakdown of institutions among the four defining megatrends of the next two decades.[7] One effect of this has been a return to closer coordination between national industry and state institutions in the pursuit of national economic interests. The convergence of economic and geostrategic goals is having a

---

[7]See National Intelligence Council. (2012). *Global Trends 2030: Alternative Worlds* (Report) Retrieved from: http://info.publicintelligence.net/GlobalTrends2030.pdf (June 1st, 2014).

transformative impact on diplomacy and its institutions. The U.S. State Department, for example, has recognized the strategic role of economic statecraft as one of the principal tenets of foreign policy in its Quadrennial Diplomacy and Development Review (QDDR), and the department has established an office of chief economist.[8] Secretary John Kerry summarized this trend in his January 2013 confirmation testimony, stating: "More than ever, foreign policy is economic policy."[9]

For the United States and Europe, the TTIP is at the heart of a reorientation in which the primacy of economics equals and, in some cases, supplants security concerns as a top geostrategic priority. Both the United States and EU recognize the TTIP as the principle policy vehicle through which they can pool their economic weight in the services of political preferences. The U.S.-European regulatory relationship has long suffered from the narcissism of petty differences. As the world's only regulatory hegemons, each has sought to win adherents to the sectoral rules governing relations with their trading partners. While this could place the U.S. and EU on the same side of a standard or a regulatory philosophy, it has often pitted the two against each other. In areas from accounting standards to the use of herbicides and drought-resistant crop seeds, the United States and EU have engaged in a regulatory "great game" in which each side imposes exclusive usage of its standards on states with which they sign FTAs.

At the same time, the size and insularity of these regulatory hegemons often creates unintended consequences for economic partners. Often, the assumption of universality leads to extraterritorial effects within the transatlantic economic corridor and with third countries that prove difficult to reconcile with domestic law. In the U.S., the implementation of the Volcker rule and regulation of derivatives by the Dodd-Frank Act has led to friction with European banking systems.[10] In the EU, European aviation-emissions requirements have led

---

[8]See US State Department. (2010). *Leading through Civilian Power: The First Quadrennial Diplomacy and Development Review*. (Report). Retrieved from: http://www.state.gov/documents/organization/153108.pdf (June 1st, 2014).

[9]Council on Foreign Relations. (24 January, 2013). *Senator John Kerry's Confirmation Hearing Statement*. (Speech). Retrieved from: http://www.cfr.org/elections/senator-john-kerrys-confirmation-hearing-statement-january-2013/p29874 (June 1st, 2014).

[10]See Gandel, S. (21 March, 2012). European Banks Try to Get Around Dodd-Frank. *CNN Money*. Retrieved from: http://finance.fortune.cnn.com/2012/03/21/europea-banks-dodd-frank/ (June 1st, 2014).

to major disputes in the airline industry over future airspace regulations.[11] Such disputes undermine the potential of the United States and EU to work as a regulatory alliance—an "economic NATO" as it has been dubbed by some proponents—that would coordinate more systematically on such issues.

The Doha round of WTO negotiations is the most apparent case in which plurilateral agreements like TTIP could be used to dislodge protracted stalemates in the multilateral order. The WTO has not significantly updated its agreement architecture since 1994. In the two decades since, the ossification of decision-making within the WTO has created an opening for plurilateral trade agreements. These trade blocs, if properly used, can serve as catalysts for greater consensus in multilateral fora such as the WTO. This logic has led several European countries that were once the most ardent champions of a strictly multilateral strategy, such as the Dutch and the Swedish, to explore alternatives, such as TTIP, more earnestly. This enhanced cooperation among like-minded states has had successes (e.g., Agreement on Government Procurement) and failures (e.g., Anti-Counterfeiting Trade Agreement). The U.S. and the EU's ability to harness the combined weight of their economic power to maintain the reins of global economic agenda-setting could, in time, allow TTIP to develop into a Global Agreement on Trade and Tariffs (GATT) 2.0. Emerging markets such as Indonesia have already stated that a U.S.-EU economic deal could re-ignite the urgency on their part to redouble their commitment to multilateral cooperation on trade. In effect, the U.S.-EU agreement could serve the same role that the North American Free Trade Agreement (NAFTA) served during the Uruguay Round: making significant global players see that it is in their interest to prevent talks from stalling. The modest agreement on customs facilitation at the December 2013 Bali WTO ministerial provides evidence of this process.

The pull of the mega-free trade agreement (FTA) strategy, of which TTIP is at the center, has also led to normative changes in bilateral negotiating strategies of some of the international economic system's most important and, at times, most recalcitrant, rising powers. Of these, China is the most important, the country who economic rise

---

[11]See Bertelsmann Foundation. (December 2012). *In the Air: International Aviation-Emissions Regulation.* (CapitolWire Report). Retrieved from: http://www.bfna.org/sites/default/files/CapitolWire%20Dec%202012.pdf (June 1st, 2014).

could prove most destabilizing. TTIP and other mega-FTAs like the Trans-Pacific Partnership could compel China to be more economically accommodating. Evidence of this already exists. In the summer of 2013, the United States and China were able to re-launch discussions on a bilateral investment treaty (BIT) at the U.S.-China Strategic and Economic Dialogue (SED). The process had been stalled since 2008 due to Beijing's insistence on continuing major restrictions on U.S. investment in China. These restrictions limited FDI to particular sectors and forced joint ventures in others, such as financial services and motor vehicles, where technology transfers are often required.[12] In a dramatic concession on the part of the Chinese, negotiations will use a "negative-list" approach to restricted sections. This means that all sectors would be open to inbound FDI unless explicitly excluded. At the same time, the Chinese and the EU have also agreed to launch Bilateral Investment Treaty (BIT) talks.[13] The Chinese have also become more willing to address restrictive practices regarding procurement contracts. The Brazilians, too, have intensified their campaign for an FTA with the EU, either within Mercosur or bilaterally. Negotiations between the EU and Mercosur started in 1999 but have stalled for years. Seeing ongoing protectionism among its fellow Mercosur member states, particularly Argentina, Brazil is pursuing alternative avenues that would allow it to codify its relationship with the EU.[14]

The attractiveness of the TTIP format has also caused concern among some of the countries most deeply integrated into the transatlantic economic corridor, specifically Turkey, Mexico and Canada. The world's 17th, 14th and 11th largest economies, whose economic viability is inexorably linked to the United States and the EU, would like to see a more permeable TTIP+3 process.[15] Turkey in particular has expressed

---

[12]Dyer, G. (July 12, 2013). Sino-US Investment Deal Sought. *Financial Times*. Retrieved from: http://www.ft.com/intl/cms/s/0/83094a3e-ea76-11e2-913c-00144feabdc0.html?siteedition=intl (June1st, 2014).

[13]Anderlini, J. (November 21, 2013). China and EU Agree to Talks on Bilateral Investment Treaty. *Financial Times*. Retrieved from: http://www.ft.com/intl/cms/s/0/2aade424-529c-11e3-8586-00144feabdc0.html (June 1st, 2014).

[14]Rathbone, J.P. & Leahy, J. (August 11, 2012). Brazil Reaches out to EU for Trade Deal. *Financial Times*. Retrieved from: http://www.ft.com/intl/cms/s/0/ca912164-0291-11e3-a9e2-00144feab7de.html#axzz2qbEAZOoX (June 1st, 2014).

[15]Barker, T. (July 17, 2013). On the "Outs": An Early Geo-economics Conundrum for the US-EU Trade Deal. *IP-Journal*. Retrieved from: https://ip-journal.dgap.org/en/ip-journal/topics/outs (June 1st, 2014).

concern that its exclusion from TTIP talks could lead to substantially asymmetric market access and put it at a disadvantage as a result of its customs union with the EU. The United States, interested in preserving Turkish cooperation across a number of geostrategic fronts in the Middle East, has attempted to assuage any perception of Turkey's exclusion through a series of joint economic projects. The U.S.-Turkey High-Level Committee, an institutional working group aimed at providing Turkey with a consultation mechanism to TTIP negotiations, is the most prominent.[16] The Turks, themselves, perceive this as a scoping exercise for a bilateral U.S.-Turkish FTA similar to the U.S.-EU High Level Working Group that eventually green-lighted the launch of TTIP negotiations. Asymmetry of interest places the U.S. in an advantageous negotiating position. The U.S. Trade Representative has already made it clear that certain confidence-building measures, such as greater intellectual property rights (IPR) protection and pricing issues related to pharmaceuticals, would need to be addressed before the formal launch of U.S.-Turkey talks.

Finally, the U.S. shale-gas revolution is changing the global energy dynamic and re-casting the interest of Central European states in a trade deal. U.S. law restricts American exports of liquefied natural gas (LNG) to only those that have an FTA with the United States. Exports to others, including the EU, are subject to a cumbersome inter-agency approval process. The International Energy Agency (IEA) has warned that without opening its market to greater exports, the U.S.'s gas boom could be faced with a demand bottleneck that will suppress exploration. There have been attempts to provide exemptions for NATO allies—legislation sponsored by former Senator Richard Lugar (R-IN) is one example of this. There are doubts, however, that this would be WTO-compliant. Countries from Spain to Lithuania have already begun developing LNG import terminals in anticipation of the global shale-gas boom led by the United States.[17] Completion of a comprehensive economic deal is an elegant way to unlock the transatlantic energy market that will maintain U.S. LNG prices at a

---

[16]See Tattersall, N. (May 16, 2013). Turkey Seeks Seat at US-EU Trade Table. *Reuters*. Retrieved from: http://www.reuters.com/article/2013/05/17/us-turkey-usa-trade-idUSBRE94F1CA20130517 (June 1st, 2014).

[17]See Bradley, B. (November 19, 2013). Lithuanian LNG Terminal Gets EU Approval, Klaipedos Nafta Says. *Bloomberg News*. Retrieved from: http://www.bloomberg.com/news/2013-11-19/lithuanian-lng-terminal-gets-eu-approval-klaipedos-nafta-says.html (June 1st, 2014).

level that encourages domestic shale exploration while providing Europe a strategic partner in the diversification of energy supply, a leading foreign-policy goal of countries whose preponderant dependence on Russia has been a source of decade-long anxiety.

Exploring TTIP's Economic Consequences

Beyond examining the TTIP's potential geopolitical significance, it is important to establish the agreement's potential main street dividends for American and European citizens in terms of GDP growth and gains in the job market. While its potential to affect the normative behavior of rising economic powers has already been demonstrated, the TTIP's ultimate success or failure will rest on its ability to yield economic benefits that are equitably distributed and outweigh the distortive effects that come from increased intra-Atlantic competition. As EU Trade Commissioner Karel De Gucht has repeatedly stated, both sides must keep their "eyes on the prize."[18] First and foremost, this means increased domestic growth and employment opportunities.

The Potential Economic Impact in the United States

A recent study, entitled *TTIP and the Fifty States*, looks at the potential impact of TTIP on the 50 U.S. states in terms of trade in goods and services. The study uses the general equilibrium modeling employed by the Center for Economic Policy Research (CEPR) and a comprehensive dataset of state-by-state exports to examine how TTIP would affect economic growth and job gains in each of the 50 states at the point of full implementation. The study defines a comprehensive scenario as a 100 percent reduction in tariffs, a 25 percent reduction in non-tariff and technical barriers to trade and a 50 percent reduction in procurement barriers.[19] It is important to note that the study does not look at the impact of TTIP on investment flows into the United States.

---

[18]European Commission. (2013). EU and US Conclude Second Round of TTIP Negotiations in Brussels. (Press Release). Retrieved from: http://europa.eu/rapid/press-release_IP-13-1091_en.htm (June 1st, 2014).

[19]For a comprehensive explanation of the methodology, see: Bertelsmann Foundation, Atlantic Council of the United States, & the British Embassy to the USA. (2013). *TTIP and the Fifty States: Jobs and Growth from Coast to Coast*. (Report). Retrieved from: http://www.bfna.org/publication/ttip-and-the-fifty-states-jobs-and-growth-from-coast-to-coast (June 1st, 2014).

The study finds that all 50 states would gain in terms of increased exports and net jobs gains. Annual exports to Europe are estimated to jump 33 percent per state, on average.[20] Trade in goods, particularly advanced manufacturing, also stand to benefit more from an ambitious TTIP than trade in services. But the greatest gains in exports to Europe occur in states that are particularly well integrated into the supply chains of the transatlantic motor vehicles market. South Carolina, a leader in this area, would see a 187 percent increase in exports to Europe,[21] followed by Alabama with a 138 percent increase[22] and Michigan with a 95 percent increase.[23]

The effects of a fully implemented TTIP on U.S. job growth are similarly positive with all states. TTIP is estimated to produce on average one new job for every 160 jobs currently in existence. That is more than 740,000 American jobs or about the equivalent of the entire working population of West Virginia or New Hampshire.[24] The top four states expected to gain in terms of absolute number of TTIP-related jobs are California, Texas, New York and Florida. California alone is expected to add approximately 75,000 jobs to its economy.[25] These states have the largest populations and work forces in the U.S. and as a result, stand to see the largest increase in TTIP-reliant jobs. But the states where TTIP has the greatest per capita impact on the job market are states with smaller populations. Nevada, Hawaii, Washington, West Virginia, Montana and Maine are expected to see the largest proportional increase in their labor force as a result of TTIP.[26]

TTIP-related job growth has two primary sources. The first is the more intuitive direct impact on the labor market. Greater exports will lead to greater jobs in a particular sector to meet greater demand. But the larger source of U.S. job growth is less intuitive, stemming from the indirect impact on the labor market. A TTIP would increase welfare and drive down prices, which would allow for greater expenditure

---

[20]Ibid., p.3.
[21]Ibid., p.41.
[22]Ibid., p. 8.
[23]Ibid., p. 23.
[24]Ibid., p. 2.
[25]Ibid., p. 12.
[26]Ibid., p.20, 27.

at the household, firm and government levels. Because the United States is a primarily service-based economy, increased disposable income leads to growth primarily in the services sector. As a result, TTIP-reliant job growth takes place primarily in the services sector while export increases occur primarily in manufacturing.

The Potential Economic Impact in Europe

In Europe, the TTIP's potential impact is similarly positive. A study by the Bertelsmann Stiftung and the IFO Institute simulates the effects of TTIP on international trade flows and labor market demand under a tariff reduction scenario and a broader comprehensive scenario under which all Non-Tariff Barriers (NTBs) are eliminated.[27] The model employed in this study differs from the one used in the prior study examining effects on U.S. states in that it combines a computational general equilibrium model with scenario modeling based on empirical evidence of the effects of tariff and NTB reduction on long term economic welfare in past comprehensive regional trade agreements. It uses this modeling to examine the impact of TTIP on long-term percentage change in GDP per capita.[28]

The study predicts social welfare gains in all member-states of the European Union in both the tariff-based and comprehensive scenarios. The study shows that per capita income will increase by 5 percent on average in the comprehensive scenario.[29] That said, there is a significant degree of variability between EU member-states. With an increase of almost 10 percent of GDP per capita, the UK stands to benefit most greatly in this model. The small open economies of the Baltics are estimated among the other large beneficiaries.

Interestingly, the study also demonstrates above average gains for states most affected by the Eurozone crisis. Of these, Spain and Ireland particularly stand out. Spain is slated to add 6.6 percent GDP per capita in the long term, attributable to a comprehensive TTIP. Ireland

---

[27]For the full report, see: Bertelsmann Stiftung & The IFO Institute. (2013). *Transatlantic Trade and Investment Partnership (TTIP): Who Benefits from a Free Trade Deal?* (Report). Retrieved from: http://www.bfna.org/sites/default/files/TTIP-GED%20study%2017June%202013.pdf (June 1st, 2014).

[28]Ibid., p.5.

[29]Ibid., p.24.

is also estimated to add 6.9 percent.[30] Both countries will also see drops in unemployment, with estimated drops of 0.62 percent in Spain and 0.84 percent in Ireland.[31] The marginal reduction in the unemployment rate is generally related to the level of unemployment in the country.[32] The states with the most limited relative welfare gains in this model are France and the Benelux countries. These countries stand to see a long term GDP per capita increase of 2.6 percent accompanied by modest decreases in unemployment (France at 0.43 percent; the Netherlands at 0.34 percent; and Belgium at 0.08 percent).[33]

One of the more controversial aspects of this study has been its analysis of third country effects that could result from TTIP. This study looks at the change across 126 countries.[34] This study is unique in that it draws attention to the third country effects, including substitution effects that potentially deep free trade agreement could cause states such as Canada, Mexico and Turkey that enjoy the greatest level of integration with the transatlantic economic corridor. This analysis does not take into account the adjustment strategies that states and firms would pursue in these "outs" in order to mitigate the TTIP's negatively distortive impact. These strategies could include the whole-sale adoption of standards and regulations or rules of origin changes that could unilaterally bring these economies in tighter alignment with the TTIP economies.[35]

It is important to note the limitations of such modeling exercises. These scenarios project potential economic dynamics decades in advance of their occurrence. Other interacting variables including changes in technology, political instability, concurrent economic phenomena in the trade and financial order and demographic trends will each inform the outcome of TTIP and implementation of other trade liberalization efforts. Nevertheless, such studies are useful as thought

---

[30]Ibid., p.. 30

[31]Ibid., p. 36.

[32]Ibid., p. 37

[33]Ibid., p.39

[34]Ibid., p.27

[35]Barker, T. (June 17, 2013). On the "Outs": An Early Geoeconomic Conundrum for the US-EU Trade Deal. *Internationale Politik Journal*. Retrieved from: https://ip-journal.dgap.org/en/ip-journal/topics/outs

exercises that focus policy-makers on the general trends that TTIP would usher in for the U.S. and European economies.

The Role of Trade Adjustment and Equitable Distribution of TTIP's Gains

The TTIP's potential impact on transatlantic economic growth and geo-economic power projection is clear. To remain politically palatable to the broad swath of constituencies necessary for its success on both sides of the Atlantic, the TTIP, and its champions, must include a social component that assures the equitable distribution of the gains in a way that creates more cohesive economies.

The notion of couching open and competitive market access within a social contract that attempts to mitigate forces that tear at social cohesion is known as embedded liberalism. The term was first employed by political scientist, John Ruggie, to describe the paradox that the coexistence of two seemingly oppositional forces—open markets centered on free trade and investment, and state-based domestic welfare distribution and employment programs—were at the heart of the political bargain that governed advanced industrial economies for much of the post-war era.[36] In the United States and most of Europe, the concept of embedded liberalism came under siege in the later Cold War era and early post-Cold War era. Even in Germany, the country whose concept of the social-market economy served as a model, it came under pressure to retrofit and, in some cases, roll back its central elements, including labor-market and unemployment reform.

In the current policy climate, however, the debate about economic equality and social cohesion is alive in the United States and Europe. President Obama's December 2011 speech in Osawatomie, Kansas was a full-throated call for a return to an economic model that balances unfettered competition with a draft of public policies aimed at correcting any concentrations of wealth resulting from previous market reforms. From maintenance of long-term unemployment benefits to increases in federal and state minimum wages, the Obama administration has put income inequality at the heart of its legislative

---

[36]Ruggie, J. (Spring 1982). International Regimes, Transactions, and Change: Embedded Liberalism in the Post-War Economic Order. *International Regimes, Vol.36, No. 2.* pp. 379-415.

agenda.[37] Germany, the EU's undisputed top economic performer, named the rising gap between the rich and poor as its top economic concern, according to a 2013 Pew survey.[38]

This question will certainly arise in policy debates about TTIP. Both sides of the Atlantic can draw on lessons from previous initiatives aimed at liberalizing the global market. The United States has more recent experience with policies meant to counteract the distortive effects of free-trade deals and distribute their welfare gains across society. Trade-adjustment assistance (TAA) is the principal fiscal stabilizing mechanism to address the displacement effects of greater openness to trade. TAA is directly targeted towards U.S. jobs and sectors that have been displaced or eliminated as a result of FTAs. The assistance has targeted programs at workers, firms and agriculture. The Department of Labor estimates that in 2010 $975 million in TAA federal funds was granted to states for programs that covered 227,882 workers. TAA seeks to address sectors of society most vulnerable to globalization. Many TAA participants include workers without a high-school education and those formerly employed in manufacturing. The average age of a worker receiving TAA worker is 46, with 12 years' experience in the displaced position.[39]

The U.S. TAA experience has been mixed. The geographic and sectoral effects are varied. TAA has played a significant role in recent efforts to forge a pro-free-trade consensus in the United States. Congressional Democrats seek to tie the passage of Trade Promotion Authority (TPA) to the passage of TAA as a means of balancing gains from trade. TAA is set to expire at the end of 2014. Addressing some of the TAA's past deficiencies to account for new sectors and patterns of labor will be important. Coupling a reformed TAA with TPA could be a means of addressing some of the imbalances that arise in the course of implementing President Obama's ambitious trade agenda.

---

[37]Halloran, L. (January 6, 2014). Democrats Tackle Politics of Income Inequality. *NPR*. Retrieved from: http://www.npr.org/blogs/itsallpolitics/2014/01/06/260267333/democrats-tackle-politics-of-income-inequality (June1st, 2014).

[38]Pew Research Center. (May 13, 2013). *The New Sick Man of Europe: the European Union*. (Report). Retrieved from: http://www.pewglobal.org/2013/05/13/chapter-1-dispirited-over-national-conditions/ (June1st, 2014).

[39]United States Department of Labor (June 22, 2012). *What is Trade Adjustment Assistance?* (Fact Sheet). *Retrieved from:* http://www.doleta.gov/tradeact/factsheet.cfm (June 1st, 2014).

While the EU system lacks the potential for fiscal transfers that undergird the U.S. system, limited adjustments for trade exist. The European Globalization Adjustment Fund (EGF), an EU financial pool set up in 2007 to provide member states with financial support for employees displaced by trade deals, provides one possible model.[40] EGF could be optimized across the EU. Currently, applications for EGF support come primarily from member states that are better placed for trade competition, such as the UK, Germany and the Netherlands. Moreover, the EGF has been made accessible to member states that are addressing youth unemployment and other aspects of the eurozone crisis. At the same time, it has been difficult to make the program more accessible to SMEs and to increase access for workers in vulnerable sectors in member states hardest hit by the economic downturn, such as Greece, Italy and Spain. And the EGF's financing was cut from €500 to €150 million a year in the EU 2014-2020 budget negotiations. Leaders could explore restoring funding to previous levels and pursuing a more efficient dissemination of EGF that works in tandem with the EU's trade agenda.

Negotiations that led to the successful launch of the SEA also provide useful policy lessons that address the TTIP's social-justice implications. In SEA negotiations, some worried that greater liberalization would augment the geographical and sectoral divides, and increase the economic disparity between a richer core and poorer periphery. Countries such as Greece, Portugal and Ireland made their support for the SEA conditional on using structural and cohesion funds as fiscal stabilizers that would offset competition from the single market.[41] This type of social bargain could again be employed to lubricate TTIP's successful passage in the Council and the European Parliament.

The Big Picture

TTIP's potentially transformative impact on domestic economic growth, reform and international geo-economic power projection is

---

[40]See European Commission. (2014). *European Globalization Adjustment Fund (EFG)*. Retrieved from: http://ec.europa.eu/social/main.jsp?catId=326& (June1st, 2014).

[41]Lodge, J. (March 1986). The Single European Act: Towards a New Euro-Dynamism? *Journal of Common Market Studies*. Vol. 24, p. 33.

predicated on the success of U.S. and EU negotiators to secure a comprehensive agreement, an assumption that is by no means guaranteed. Traditional transatlantic disputes that have hindered past cooperation, particularly around the use of GMOs, geographic indicators (GIs) and sanitary and phytosanitary (SPS) measures, will continue to daunt negotiations. Moreover, they have been joined by three new fault lines that represent the heart of the transatlantic economy and have occupied significant space in U.S. and EU public policy since the 2008 crisis.

The first is financial services regulation. A byproduct of their histories, the U.S. and EU banking and financial services sectors have followed divergent institutional development pathways that, in an area of global banking, can lead to unintended competitive advantages or disadvantages when not carefully regulated. Since the 2008 global financial crisis, the United States and the EU have coordinated closely in numerous multilateral forums, from the Financial Stability Board to the G20, to create broad guidelines for the re-regulation of the financial sector. That said, more granular regulatory reform, stemming from the implementation of the 2010 Dodd-Frank Act in the U.S. and the piecemeal legislative effort in the EU, has created a potential backsliding on G20 commitments and led to a patchwork of extraterritorial agreements that could ultimately fragment the transatlantic financial sector. The U.S. administration, particularly the Treasury, regulators such as the U.S. Commodity Futures Trading Commission (CFTC), and some members of Congress have proved reluctant to include financial-services regulation in TTIP negotiations. They fear the possibility that consultations on the subject will be used as an opportunity to re-litigate issues addressed in Dodd-Frank.

The second fault line is public procurement. Procurement expenditure comprises 16 percent of total GDP in the EU and roughly 12 percent in the United States.[42] Its usage touches on some of the most highly valued manufacturing and services sectors of the economy, from aerospace to sophisticated medical technology. The United

---

[42]For public procurement statistics in the EU, see: http://ec.europa.eu/trade/policy/accessing-markets/public-procurement/ (June1st, 2014). For public procurement statistics in the United States, see: OECD (2011). "Size of Public Procurement Market" in *Government at a Glance 2011*. (Report). Retrieved from: http://www.oecdilibrary.org/docserver/download/4211011ec046.pdf?expires=1389193730&id=id&accname=guest&checksum=34139E347C08B1876E69A8DD56DC4DC2 (June 1st, 2014).

States and EU member states are bound by the WTO's Global Procurement Agreement (GPA), which guarantees reciprocal access to national procurement markets.[43] Yet, America's unique federal structure provides states autonomous control of their expenditure. This has led to the proliferation of states' "Buy America" provisions whose effects ultimately exclude European companies and other foreign firms from state contracts, even when projects are funded by federal block grants. The EU, in particular, will look to a TTIP agreement as a vehicle to broaden guarantees for reciprocal access to public-procurement markets at the state and local levels.[44]

The third fault line is the information and communication technology (ICT) sector. In the past decade, ICT has been a primary driver of transatlantic economic growth, particularly for the United States. Four out of the 10 largest U.S. companies by market capitalization (Apple, Microsoft, Google and GE) are in the ICT sector, which stands to gain more than almost any other U.S. sector from the TTIP in terms of the elimination of and protection from non-tariff barriers to trade.[45] The NSA revelations concerning the use of U.S. companies as mechanisms for gathering intelligence data, however, have intensified the scrutiny of cross-border data flows and agreements, such as Safe Harbor, that undergird the budding ICT marketplace.[46] The revelations underscored a long-existent ambivalence in certain European member states and in the European Parliament of the sector's business model, which is reliant on users to provide data as a de facto "fee for service."[47] The policy discussions surrounding TTIP will have signifi-

---

[43]See: *The WTO Plurilateral Agreement on Government Procurement (GPA)*. Retrieved from: http://www.wto.org/english/tratop_e/gproc_e/gp_gpa_e.htm (June 1st, 2014).

[44]See Politi, J. (June 26, 2013). Buy America Laws Raise Hurdles in European Talks. *Financial Times*. Retrieved from: http://www.ft.com/intl/cms/s/0/0e83d6e6-dd76-11e2-a756-00144 feab7de.html#axzz2poRKEH3n (June 1st, 2014).

[45]See Paoletta, P. (2013). ICT in the TTIP – An Opportunity to Enhance Services Trade & Cybersecurity. *The European Institute*. Retrieved from: http://www.europeaninstitute.org/EA-May-2013/ict-in-the-ttip-an-opportunity-to-enhance-services-trade-and-cybersecurity.html (June 1st, 2014).

[46]See Scott, M. (November, 27, 2013). Europe Urges US to Handle Data Privacy with Care. *The New York Times*. Retrieved from: http://www.nytimes.com/2013/11/28/business/international/europe-urges-us-to-handle-data-privacy-with-care.html?_r=0 (June 1st, 2014).

[47]German chancellor Angela Merkel has stated that Europe should see ICT as a strategic economic sector, similar to what it does with Airbus and Galileo. Estonian President Toomas Ilves has called for the creation of a European cloud computing network wholly separate

cant impact on the business models of the U.S. ICT sector and the openness of the transatlantic digital economy. Other next-generation sticking points, such as the investor state dispute settlement (ISDS) and divergent fuel-quality standards, are sensitive areas that could also become potential spoilers in negotiations.

Involved stakeholders, particularly those in the U.S. Congress and the European Parliament who will have to vote on an eventual agreement, will quickly be drawn to the narrow interests for which collective action can be mobilized most easily. TTIP negotiators will need to maintain strategic focus on a deal's net geopolitical, economic and social dividends to reach an ambitious but achievable agreement. Shaping a communication strategy that transcends the sector-specific regulatory issues and instead draws attention to TTIP's strategic objectives will be central to successfully concluding an agreement.[48] TTIP's strategic value can be hard to grasp in tangible terms, but it ultimately provides the most convincing evidence that its pursuit is worth the difficulties.

---

from existing US cloud services. The EU's cybersecurity strategy calls for the Euro R&D fund to be used to create an indigenous industrial base.

[48]See Luce, E. (December 8, 2013). Obama Cannot Lead from Behind on Trade. *Financial Times*. Retrieved from: http://www.ft.com/intl/cms/s/0/a74df46e-5d1a-11e3-a558-00144fe-abdc0.html#axzz2poRKEH3n (June 1st, 2014).

Chapter 10

Science Diplomacy:
Transatlantic Asset and Competition

Tom C. Wang

When Benjamin Franklin was sent to Paris as America's first ambassador, he was already well-known in France and elsewhere in Europe as the American scientist who experimented with electricity and lightning. In the Age of Enlightenment, Franklin's scientific accomplishments offered him entry into French society. Science diplomacy—an expression, which has acquired use over the past decade—has been practiced at least since the founding of the United States. For the better part of the last four centuries, science, as a source of Soft Power, was more commonly demonstrated in Europe, which was the pre-eminent scientific region that drew foreign scientists from all over the world, including the United States. The first American Nobel Laureate, Albert Michelson, who received the 1907 prize in physics, studied at the Universities of Berlin and Heidelberg as well as visited the College de France and École Polytechnique in Paris.

Modern science diplomacy established itself, if not in name, then by action, following World War II, and especially during the Cold War. Because of their histories, the United States and Europe (this paper focuses primarily at the European Union level of analysis) have taken different approaches to the use of science in support of broader foreign policy objectives. The two economies have developed complementary but different competences in science diplomacy reflecting European integration priorities and U.S. geopolitical ones. Scientific activities, including higher education in the sciences and engineering, are important tools of soft power for the two economies and will continue to be so in the future. Today, the U.S. and European approaches to science diplomacy are converging. Concurrently, science diplomacy will increasingly be a source of transatlantic competition.

Science Diplomacy and Soft Power

A country's science and technology system and culture can be, in itself and as a driver of economic vibrancy, a source of soft power, which has been treated extensively by Nye and others.[1] The strength of such power depends not only on the quality, size, and prestige of a country's scientific system but also includes the enabling mechanisms and policies for accessing the system, including immigration policies and openness of higher education and scientific training institutions.

Science for diplomacy, or simply *science diplomacy*, describes the use of scientific activities (e.g., international joint research, academic exchange programs, etc.) as a soft power tool. Governments can wield it to further foreign policy objectives. For example, governments may develop policies and mechanisms that facilitate engagement of its scientific community with that of a targeted country in the form of formal intergovernmental science and technology agreements or the establishment of special funding programs for joint research. No less important, civil society, including non-governmental organizations, can wield science diplomacy to support the broader relationship between societies.

Other areas at the intersection of science and diplomacy, while not treated in this paper, are important aspects of U.S. and E.U. relationships between each other and with other countries and regions. These other areas include:[2] the scientific or technical aspects of formal diplomatic apparatus and processes (e.g., in negotiations of environmental and arms control agreements) and the employment of diplomatic apparatus and processes for scientific purposes (e.g., mega-scale, multinational scientific experiments and research infrastructures, like the International Thermonuclear Experimental Reactor organization (ITER) or the International Space Station).

---

[1]See for example: Nye, J. S. (2004). *Soft Power*. New York: Public Affairs.
[2]The Royal Society/AAAS (2010). *New Frontiers in Science Diplomacy*. London: The Royal Society.

Contrasting Approaches:
Cold War Geopolitics versus Regional Integration

The most oft-cited examples of modern U.S. science diplomacy are its use during three decades of the Cold War—involving Japan, the Soviet Union, and the People's Republic of China.[3] These science diplomacy activities took place firmly within the U.S. geo-political lens: ensuring a solid ally in Japan for the Western-most bulwark against the Communist bloc, countering the Soviets while avoiding a global nuclear war, and reinforcing Sino-Soviet rivalries. U.S. science diplomacy hinged on a strong and vibrant scientific environment fed by the hot and cold wars of the mid-twentieth century, the relatively open and mobile (though at times, and for specific societal groups, highly restrictive) society, earlier investments in higher education (e.g., the Land Grant Acts), and the country's global draw as the leader of the free world. The U.S. approach to science diplomacy can be described as active, direct, and outwardly-focused.

While U.S. science diplomacy efforts were outwardly focused on global geopolitics, European science diplomacy had an important inward component that supported the European regional integration agenda and its related goal of strengthening economic competitiveness. One of the major examples of science diplomacy in the second half of the twentieth century is the project to create the European Center for Nuclear Research, better known by its French acronym CERN. It brought together former adversaries of World War II to work together to rebuild excellence in physics in Europe.[4] Other post-World War II examples abound, including the European Atomic Energy Community (Euratom), which sought to coordinate nuclear energy research and development, standards, and supplies or the European Molecular Biology Laboratory (EMBL), which sought to do for European biology what CERN did for physics. Not coincidentally, the importance of science as a bonding agent within Europe paralleled the efforts to tie together the economic future of Europe, from the European Coal and Steel Community to the European Union of

[3]Neureiter, N. P.; Turekian, V. C. (2012). Science and Diplomacy: The Past as Prologue. *Science & Diplomacy*, 1(1): 5-11. URL: http://www.sciencediplomacy.org/editorial/2012/science-and-diplomacy (last accessed: June 1st, 2014).

[4]http://public.web.cern.ch/public/en/about/History54-en.html (last accessed: June 1st, 2014).

today. Following the fall of the Berlin Wall, and the collapse of the Iron Curtain, science diplomacy was an instrument to begin to bring in the Eastern European states into the European project. The European Commission provided support to scientists in the East (e.g. Programme of Community Aid to the Countries of Central and Eastern Europe (PHARE)) and the intergovernmental organization European Cooperation in Science and Technology (COST) began admitting members from the former Warsaw Pact as early as 1991.[5] The 1993 Maastricht Treaty, which officially brought forth the name "European Union" (EU) and set a path for the single Euro currency, stated "the Community shall have the objective of strengthening the scientific and technological bases of Community industry and encouraging it to become more competitive at international level, while promoting all the research activities deemed necessary by virtue of other Chapters of this Treaty."[6] There are many more examples at the individual European country-level. In essence, science diplomacy within Europe was tied to the modern integration of Europe with its emphasis on economic integration and competitiveness.

Converging Approaches

At the dawn of the twenty-first century, almost every part of the world is prioritizing investments in science and technology (S&T) as an engine for economic growth and prosperity. As such, science diplomacy efforts are on the rise, gaining increased political recognition, and also increasingly about supporting economic priorities. While the importance of S&T to U.S. national security, both military and economic, was well articulated during the Cold War, especially in response to Sputnik, there has been domestic concern of waning preeminence in S&T, and the need for a renewed emphasis and investment to compete in the global economy. The much publicized National Academies' report, "Rising above the Gathering Storm" captured this concern:

---

[5]Communication from the Commission to the Council and the European Parliament: Cooperation in the Field of Science and Technology Between the European Community and the Countries of Central and Eastern Europe, May 11, 1992, Brussels.
[6]Treaty on European Union (92/C 191/01), Title XV: Research and Technological Development, Article 130f.

> Although the U.S. economy is doing well today, current trends in each of those criteria indicate that the United States may not fare as well in the future without government intervention. This nation must prepare with great urgency to preserve its strategic and economic security. Because other nations have, and probably will continue to have, the competitive advantage of a low wage structure, the United States must compete by optimizing its knowledge-based resources, particularly in science and technology, and by sustaining the most fertile environment for new and revitalized industries and the well-paying jobs they bring.[7]

In President Obama's second inaugural address, he underscored the connection between S&T and U.S. economic prosperity in stating, "The path towards sustainable energy sources will be long and sometimes difficult. But America cannot resist this transition, we must lead it. We cannot cede to other nations the technology that will power new jobs and new industries; we must claim its promise. That's how we will maintain our economic vitality and our national treasure—our forests and waterways, our crop lands and snow-capped peaks."[8]

Contemporary U.S. science diplomacy efforts have continued to reflect geo-political considerations, but, as with much of post-Cold War international relations and global economic competition, they are becoming much more diffuse and diverse, economically and global-challenges-oriented. During the George W. Bush administration, science and technology efforts, though not labeled as "science diplomacy," were initiated to reach out to Africa through health assistance, especially PEPFAR (the President's Emergency Plan for AIDS Relief) and engage the global community on pandemic influenza (e.g., International Partnership on Avian and Pandemic Influenza) and even climate change issues (e.g., the Asia-Pacific Partnership on Clean Development and Climate). The current Obama administration has explicitly embraced science diplomacy with efforts such as its 2009 Cairo Initiative and the Science Envoy program that can serve geopo-

---

[7]National Academies Committee on Prospering in the Global Economy of the 21st Century (2007). *Rising Above The Gathering Storm: Energizing and Employing America for a Brighter Future.* Washington: National Academies Press.

[8]http://www.whitehouse.gov/the-press-office/2013/01/21/inaugural-address-president-barack-obama (last accessed: June 1st, 2014).

litical priorities.[9] It has also engaged in efforts that support U.S. economic and energy security priorities, for example, in launching the U.S.-China Clean Energy Research Center in 2009.

Europe is increasingly outwardly looking in its scientific cooperation, in spite of the euro crisis and threats of EU fragmentation. The EU's mechanism for funding multilateral research, the just completed Seventh Framework Program, and its newly launched 80 billion euro successor "Horizon 2020," places specific importance on research cooperation with third countries (i.e. countries outside the Union). New EU policies explicitly harness science diplomacy: "*Science diplomacy* will use international cooperation in research and innovation as an instrument of soft power and a mechanism for improving relations with key countries and regions. Good international relations may, in turn, facilitate effective cooperation in research and innovation."[10] In certain cases, support for international S&T cooperation and capacity-building could assist European geopolitical priorities, such as in the Middle East Peace Process.[11]

Competition Exacerbated, Cooperation Needed

The U.S. and the EU have clear competitive advantages in the use of science diplomacy compared with much of the world, though they are becoming less differentiated, and in certain cases diminishing. U.S. science diplomacy has benefited from a large, deep, and diverse scientific community of people and institutions, funding and policies. Besides being a source of new scientific ideas, innovative technologies, and high-margin products, the United States has been able to attract the best minds in students and technical professionals from all over the world. The United States has benefited from its historical competitive advantage in S&T from its early investment in the basic sciences, relatively

[9]http://www.whitehouse.gov/administration/eop/ostp/sciencediplomacy (last accessed: June 1st, 2014).

[10]Communication from the Commission to the European Parliament, the Council, the European Economic and Social Committee and the Committee of the Regions "Enhancing and Focusing E.U. International Cooperation in Research and Innovation: A Strategic Approach" (COM(2012) 497) September 14, 2012, Brussels.

[11]Miller, R. (2012) Progress without Peace. *Science and Diplomacy*, 2 (2): 32-45. URL: http://www.sciencediplomacy.org/article/2013/progress-without-peace (last accessed: June 1st, 2014).

open immigration policies, coupling of higher education and research, prosperous economy, stable political system, open society, and perception as an exemplar of liberty. The United States had few challengers in this regard, particularly during the Cold War. The twenty-first century is looking rather different for the United States. Not only has Europe become a vibrant, and more or less single, economy, but many parts of the former "Third World" have emerged as middle-income economies or otherwise are growing rapidly. Not only is there growth, there is substantial increased investment in S&T and to a certain extent research and education in many of these countries, particularly in Asia.[12] The post-9/11 policies that have, in part, led to the U.S. National Academies report entitled "Beyond 'Fortress America'" reflects a United States that is less, if not in actuality then in perception, open—to people, to knowledge, and to ideas.[13] And while the strengths of individual science-related government agencies are still often world-beating, their individual abilities to engage internationally are often less capable, often limited by the oversight of a domestically-oriented Congress. Moreover, the collective ability of U.S. science agencies to coordinate and cooperate internationally is challenging, which is often important in supporting a foreign policy agenda and science diplomacy efforts.[14]

Europe has been making progress over the course of sixty-odd years since the founding of the European Coal and Steel Community to build a Europe that can be more than the sum of its nation-state parts, minimizing those differences that are sources of conflict and synergizing differences that provide valuable diversity. There are increasingly robust and well-supported mechanisms to foster intra-European and international research through the Framework Program, and to promote basic research excellence through the European Research Council. More recently, EU ministers have agreed to implement a unitary patent system across Europe. The EU is seeking to establish a European Research Area (ERA)[15] where the knowledge

---

[12]National Science Board (2012). *Science and Engineering Indicators 2012*. Arlington VA: National Science Foundation.

[13]National Research Council (2009). *Beyond "Fortress America:" National Security Controls on Science and Technology in a Globalized World*. Washington: The National Academies Press.

[14]National Science Board (2008). *International Science and Engineering Partnerships: A Priority for U.S. Foreign Policy and Our Nation's Innovation Enterprise*. Arlington VA: National Science Foundation.

[15]http://ec.europa.eu/research/era/era_communication_en.htm (last accessed: June 1st, 2014).

goods (i.e. students, scientists, knowledge) can cross without hindrance across the EU as easily as tradable cargo and physical goods, and its success or failure may ultimately determine whether it can rival the United States in science and technology.[16]

For the United States, can it maintain its attractiveness as a place to study and work in S&T while developing new mechanisms and processes to cooperate that are based on partnerships and do not rely on brain drain to the United States? For the EU, can it take advantage of its intra-European integration experiences and mechanisms, and adapt them to work beyond Europe while making Europe an attractive place for international S&T?

For both economies, science diplomacy is becoming more complicated as a soft power tool. The United States and the EU, and not to mention other advanced economies like Japan and emerging economies like the BRIC's (Brazil, Russia, India, China and South Africa), have to compete for the best international resources (e.g., talented students, advanced research infrastructures, or wealthy scientific partners). Certainly, many cases are cooperative, win-win situations for both the United States and the EU, especially if multilateral cooperative regimes are established or available (e.g. ITER). More importantly with respect to science diplomacy, other countries now have multiple choices of scientific partner countries with whom to cooperate. The challenge for both the United States and the EU is to consider how science diplomacy is employed in the suite of other foreign policy tools, and how that science diplomacy fits into a globalized scientific environment.

The science diplomacy instrument is most effective if it is coherent and supportive of foreign policy goals and strategies. With converging national priorities focused intensively on economic prowess, more pressing global challenges, and the intensifying competitive international S&T landscape, it will be increasingly difficult for the United States and the EU to employ science diplomacy competitively in the medium to long-term. This suggests that there are new opportunities and the need for new mechanisms for multilateral engagement, with the United States and Europe working together toward shared foreign policy objectives.

---

[16]Chessa, A.; Morescalchi, A.; Pammolli, F.; Penner, O.; Petersen, A.M.; Riccaboni, M. (2013). Is Europe Evolving Toward an Integrated Research Area? *Science*, 339 (6120): 650–651.

Epilogue

The Power Debate in the Aftermath of the Annexation of Crimea

Daniel S. Hamilton and András Simonyi

Since the conception of this book, things have clearly changed in the world. We see the advances made by illiberal regimes, who are offering an alternative model to free and democratic, transparent and open societies. In Western societies, achievement does not always match aspiration. Nonetheless, we believe in the rule of law, human rights and checks and balances. Illiberal regimes do not. We believe in the fight against corruption. Illiberal regimes do not. We believe in a free press. Illiberal regimes do not. We believe in respect for the rights of the individual, irrespective of race, religion or sexual orientation. Illiberal regimes do not.

These contrasts have been sharpened by recent events. The short-lived successes of the Arab Spring have largely unraveled; an authoritarian regime was installed in Egypt through "free" elections, only to be replaced by force by an authoritarian regime of a different stripe. European extremism—an amorphous collection of anti-immigrant, anti-Semitic, anti-European and anti-American philosophies—is on the rise. Some members of the European Union, not without success, are toying with the notion of establishing de facto one-party rule, under the veil of institutions designed for democracy.

Perhaps most troubling has been the return of Vladimir Putin as president of Russia. Not that he was ever out of power. In fact, he has established an axiom: in Russia, power is where Vladimir Putin is, irrespective whether he is Prime Minister or President. He has now established a model of leadership that is based on a number of pillars. One is a strong military, capable of new kinds of military adventures and which has learned from its Georgia campaign, which almost ended in disaster for Putin. Thanks to the West's own weakness, divisions, misunderstandings and complacency, it didn't. Putin also controls of gas (and oil) supplies to a large number of democracies in Europe. He exerts full control over the Duma, which helps him maintain the illusion of democracy He has built a strong second tier of power brokers, almost all of whom come from the former KGB. Finally, he has reined in the Russian media; today hardly anything remains of the once thriving independent media outlets.

In short, Vladimir Putin has amassed a range of hard and soft power tools, and he is showing that he is adept at using them. When in February 2014 Russia decided to invade Ukraine and annex the Crimea, the campaign was well-prepared. Putin attacked a country that was weakened by internal strife, blood-letting on the Maidan, and a totally corrupted Yanukovych government. A major trade agreement between the EU and Ukraine had just fallen through and the political leaders of the West had fallen asleep. The "oooo" and "aahh" resounding through the Sochi Olympic stadium was so loud that European leaders could not hear the sound of the military build-up just a few hundred miles away. Putin also impressed a large part of the world through his RT, the English/American speaking news channel that is such an amazing fake of the original, that millions fell for it. It is so good, it takes a trained ear and eye to see the difference. By the time he sent in the "little green men," which is how his unmarked FSB troops operating in Eastern Ukraine are popularly known, he had deployed a very complex set of hard and soft-power tools. His military and his diplomacy was ready, as were his supporters in the West. He had also sabotaged alternatives to his gas supply to Europe for over a decade, and has actively built support movements in Europe and bought off leading European politicians (surprisingly cheaply).

Some are stunned at Putin's success. We shouldn't be. In many ways his success is of our own making. There is an aspect however, that we have omitted thus far. He understood something of our debates about power, and came to the conclusion, that the West is right: only a smarter use of all the tools of power will lead to success. He mastered the game while Western experts continue to debate the right name to give to the complexity of our power toolbox. Western leaders claiming to have read Joseph Nye's books on soft power apparently speed-read the parts where Nye himself warns against a one-sided approach. As we note in one of the chapters, Europe has been kidding itself with the idea that hard power is for America and soft power is for Europe. All the while, Putin put together a smarter power toolbox, in the spirit of the "spectral" concept we advance in this volume, which includes an array and gradations of both hard and soft power tools.

Meanwhile, the situation in Ukraine and the broader region continues to deteriorate. Malaysian Airlines 417 was shot down by pro-Russian separatists in eastern Ukraine. The Minsk Agreement setting forth a possible settlement has been violated so many times it appears to have little future. Russia continues to deny the direct involvement of Russian forces on Ukrainian territory to aid the separatists. Russian sorties into the airspace of a number of NATO and Partner countries continue unabated.

The European Union and America (this is our suggested order of responsibility) must continue to support the democratization of Ukraine and support the its quest for sovereignty and integrity. However, we must also draw the conclusions fast. We truly hope this crisis is also an opportunity. We hope it will push us to understand better the nature of threats to our free and democratic societies, not only from states and governments who see us as their adversary, or much worse, their enemy, but from non-state actors. The efforts by the two—state and non-state—will unfortunately collude more and more, the fundament of their agreement being that the West is the common threat to the existence of both illiberal regimes and extremists. To counter them, it is an imperative to find better, more effective, more sophisticated and of course smarter combinations of the tools at our disposal, as individual countries and as allies.

Today Americans may be waking up to the fact that they can't withdraw from the world. They are slowly reckoning with the hard truth that leadership in the free world is called for and the country that needs to take this responsibility upon itself is the United States. It does not stand alone. Most of Europe, Australia, Japan, South Korea, New Zealand and an increasing number of African and Latin American countries all share these perspectives. In the face of the threats to our way of life it is important that we accelerate debate on the ways and purposes to which in which we employ our incredibly rich treasure trove of power tools.

But we must also be careful in how we deploy these assets. Communication technology is not necessarily the friend of freedom, democracy and human rights. The Nazis used cutting edge technologies of the day to refine their propaganda, with innovations in radio broadcasting and film which worked their "deadly magic" on the masses. These tools became dreaded weapons in the hands of Stalinist propaganda as well. It is true that in the end technology was key in tearing down the iron Curtain between East and West. However, twenty five years on, we see Russia spending huge amounts on poisonous propaganda, using Western technology to influence our publics. We should not underestimate the damages it causes.

In the "war of ideologies" the internet has been a blessing and a curse: while it is a means of furthering democracy and freedom of speech, we should not underestimate the enormous challenges it poses as a means of communication for authoritarianism, extremist ideologies and policies. Democracies have become complacent and lazy. Islamic Jihadists are using Facebook, YouTube and Twitter with the same level of sophistication, with marked success, to influence young people, garner support and recruit fighters for their war on western liberal democracies. We can and should do better.

We intended this book to be part of the debate not just on a smarter use of our power resources but also a more courageous use of such resources in support of our ideals. While we do not believe that our model of society is the only possible one, we do believe that only freedom, human rights and respect for others will free up fully the most important reserves of a society: its creative people. This is something worth spending our power on.

The smarter we spend it, the more successful we will be.

Washington D.C., January 2015

About the Authors

(in alphabetical order)

Tyson Barker is the former Director for Trans-Atlantic Relations where his portfolio included the European-American economic relationship, US-EU cooperation, the Congressional European Parliament Initiative (CEPI) and tracking rising political leaders in the US and Europe. He has written for numerous publications on both sides of the Atlantic including *Foreign Affairs, Foreign Policy, Politico, the Atlantic, National Interest* and *Spiegel*.

Mr. Barker is a Truman National Security Fellow and has received fellowships from Fulbright program, Taiwan Cultural Exchange Program and the Starr Foundation. He has a bachelor's degree from Columbia University and a master's degree from The Johns Hopkins University School of Advanced International Studies (SAIS). In addition to his native English, he speaks fluent German and Spanish.

Esther Brimmer, at the time of writing, was the Assistant Secretary for International Organization Affairs, advancing U.S. interests through international organizations in areas such as human rights, peacekeeping and climate change. In her career, Dr. Brimmer served in the U.S. government in additional capacities, including as a member of the policy planning staff at the U.S. Department of State from 1999 to 2001, as a special assistant to the Under Secretary of State for Political Affairs from 1993 to 1995.

In addition to her government service, Dr. Brimmer was Deputy Director and Director of Research at the Center for Transatlantic Relations at the Johns Hopkins University's Paul H. Nitze School of Advanced International Studies (SAIS) from 2001-2009 and was a member of the SAIS faculty. She also taught at the College of Europe in Belgium. From 1995-1999 she was a Senior Associate at the Carnegie Commission on Preventing Deadly Conflict. Earlier she served on Capitol Hill as a Legislative Analyst for the Democratic Study Group in the U.S. House of Representatives. Immediately after earning her doctorate she spent two years as a management consultant with McKinsey & Company.

Dr. Brimmer has published several articles and monographs and edited eight books on transatlantic and international affairs.

Paula J. Dobriansky is a Senior Fellow at Harvard University's JFK Belfer Center for Science and International Affairs and Chair of the National Board of the World Affairs Councils of America. In 2013-14, along with former Senator John Warner and Governor Bill Richardson, she was a co-chair of the Center

---

The opinions expressed in this book are entirely of the authors and do not necessarily reflect those of any institution or government.

for a New American Security Task Force on Unconventional Energy and U.S. National Security. In February 2014, the task force report, *Energy Rush: Shale Production and U.S. National Security* was released.

Previously, Ms. Dobriansky was Senior Vice President and Global Head of Government and Regulatory Affairs from 2010 to 2012 at Thomson Reuters. She also held the Distinguished National Security Chair at the U.S. Naval Academy. From 2001-2009, Ambassador Dobriansky served as Under Secretary of State for Democracy and Global Affairs. Among her primary accomplishments, she established and led the US-India, US-China and US-Brazil Global Issues Fora, which advanced crucial work and international cooperation on environment, energy, health, development and humanitarian issues. She was also head of delegation and lead negotiator on U.S. climate change policy. In February 2007, she was appointed the President's Special Envoy to Northern Ireland. She received the Secretary of State's highest honor, the Distinguished Service Medal for her work in these positions.

Other government appointments include: Associate Director for Policy and Programs at USIA, Deputy Assistant Secretary of State for Human Rights and Humanitarian Affairs, Deputy Head of the US Delegation to the 1990 Copenhagen Conference on Security and Cooperation in Europe and Director of European and Soviet Affairs at the National Security Council, the White House. From 1997-2001, she served on the Presidentially appointed U.S. Advisory Commission on Public Diplomacy. Ambassador Dobriansky also served as Senior Vice President and Director of the Washington office of the Council on Foreign Relations and was the Council's first George F. Kennan senior fellow for Russian and Eurasian studies. She has a B.S.F.S summa cum laude from Georgetown University School of Foreign Service and an M.A. and Ph.D in Soviet political/military affairs from Harvard University.

Stacia George, at the time of writing, was a Council on Foreign Relations International Affairs Fellow with Georgetown's Institute for the Study of Diplomacy, and later served as a Principal for Government Services at Caerus Associates, applying her vast background managing projects in countries in conflict to current programs.

Ms. George has over a decade of experience managing conflict and international development projects, specializing in post-conflict and transitional environments, stabilization and counterinsurgency programming, and disarmament, demobilization, and reintegration (DDR) of former combatants. She has worked extensively with USAID's Office of Transition Initiatives (OTI), including assignments in Pakistan as OTI's Country Representative, as Deputy and Country Representative in the Democratic Republic of the Congo, and as Deputy Team Leader for OTI's program in Afghanistan. As a Senior Transition Advisor at OTI, she has also helped create and launch new country programs in Colombia, Nepal, and Sudan. Prior to joining Caerus, she studied

The opinions expressed in this book are entirely of the authors and do not necessarily reflect those of any institution or government.

U.S. counterinsurgency policies at Georgetown's Institute for the Study of Diplomacy as a Council on Foreign Relations International Affairs Fellow.

George earned an MA in International Relations and Economics with a concentration in conflict management from Johns Hopkins School of Advanced International Studies (SAIS) and a BA with honors in International Studies and Spanish from Niagara University. She is fluent in Spanish and French and speaks basic Kiswahili and Italian.

Daniel S. Hamilton is the Austrian Marshall Plan Foundation Professor and Executive Director of the Center for Transatlantic Relations at the Paul H. Nitze School of Advanced International Studies, Johns Hopkins University. He also serves as Executive Director of the American Consortium on EU Studies. Recent books include *Open Ukraine: Changing Course towards a European Future*; *The Geopolitics of TTIP*; *Transatlantic 2020: A Tale of Four Futures*, and *Europe 2020: Competitive or Complacent?* He has served in a variety of senior positions in the U.S. State Department, including as Deputy Assistant Secretary of State and Associate Director of the Secretary's Policy Planning Staff.

Aude Jehan is a Visiting Professor at the University of California Santa Barbara and a Non-Resident Fellow at the Center for Transatlantic Relations, at the Paul H. Nitze School of Advanced International Studies (SAIS) of Johns Hopkins University. She is also a Member of the Editorial Board of *EU-Topias*, a trilingual journal in Communication, Intercultural and European Studies, co-published by the University of Geneva in Switzerland and the University of Valencia in Spain.

For the last five years, Dr. Jehan has been researching and teaching both in the US and in Europe. At the time of writing, she served as French Embassy Fellow at the Center for Transatlantic Relations, investigating the Arab awakening; the political use of culture in foreign affairs; global governance and Smart Power.

In addition to her work in academia, she served at the European Parliament in 2009 and in the nonprofit sector from 2004 to 2008. She was successively Project Leader at the *Plate-forme Eurocité* of the University of Geneva and Director of Communication at the European Center of Culture in Switzerland. In this position, she organized many political and cultural events, including the Official Celebration of the 50th Anniversary of the Treaties of Rome in Switzerland, in collaboration with the European Commission and the European Council.

Dr. Jehan has received numerous awards for her research projects. She is the author of three monographs and of various articles published both in French and in English in major newspapers and journals.

The opinions expressed in this book are entirely of the authors and do not necessarily reflect those of any institution or government.

Alain Lamassoure is a French Politician and a Member of the European Parliament. Within the European Parliament he is a member of the Committee on Economic and Monetary Affairs and substitute member in the Committee on Budgets. He is also member of the Delegation for relations with the countries of South Asia. As a member of the European People's Party (EPP), he is the spokesman for the French delegation in the EPP group. At the time of writing, M. Lamassoure was also Chair of the Committee on Budgets.

Prior to his European commitment, M. Lamassoure served in the French government in various capacities. In 2005, he was Vice-President of the Cercle de l'Industrie, the forum for major French industrial firms that aims to define a new industrial policy and improve economic governance in Europe. From 2002 to 2005 he served as Vice-President of the European Movement France.

From 1993 to 1995, M. Lamassoure served as French Minister for European Affairs. In 1995 he was appointed Minister for Budget and Government spokesman. In these various capacities he was involved in the preparations for France's adoption of the euro, the 1995 enlargement, the French Presidency of the European Union (1995) and the negotiations on the Treaty of Amsterdam and the Stability Pact.

M. Lamassoure is Knight of the Legion of Honor.

Annemie Neyts-Uyttebroeck is a Belgian politician. At the time of writing, she was a member of the European Parliament, serving on the Committee on Foreign Affairs, the Subcommittee on Security and Defense, and the delegation for relations with NATO. She was also the Liberal Group spokesperson on Foreign Affairs and served as well in the delegation to the ACP-EU Joint Parliamentary Assembly.

Mrs. Neyts-Uyttebroeck previously served in the Belgian government in additional capacities, including Member of the Federal Parliament (1981-1994 and 2003-2004); Secretary of State in the Federal Government with responsibility for Greater Brussels (1981-1985); Secretary of State for European Affairs (2000-2001); Federal Minister with responsibility for European Affairs, International Trade and Agriculture (2001-2003)

Native of Flanders, she studied in French and graduated in Romance philology, then in Press and Social Communication Sciences, and graduated in teaching qualification for secondary education at the University of Brussels (VUB).

Mrs. Neyts-Uyttebroeck has received numerous honorary distinctions including Officer and Commander of the Order of Leopold in Belgium, and Knight of the Legion of Honor in France.

The opinions expressed in this book are entirely of the authors and do not necessarily reflect those of any institution or government.

Paul J. Saunders is Executive Director of the Center for the National Interest and a member of the Center's Board of Directors. He is the Center's Chief Operating Officer and directs its U.S.-Russian Relations Program in addition to leading projects on other issues, including energy and climate change and U.S.-Japan relations. He is also Associate Publisher of the foreign policy magazine *The National Interest*, published bi-monthly by the Center for the National Interest. He serves on the board of directors of the Energy Innovation Reform Project, a non-governmental organization that promotes practical policies to advance energy innovation in the United States.

Mr. Saunders served in the Bush Administration from 2003 to 2005 as Senior Advisor to the Under Secretary of State for Global Affairs. In that capacity, he worked on a broad range of transnational issues, in particular with respect to Russia, Ukraine, and the former Soviet Union, as well as Iraq, China and India.

Earlier, Mr. Saunders served as Director of the Center from 1997 to 2003, and was Assistant Director of the Center from its founding in 1994 until 1997. In 2000, he was a Senior Policy Advisor to the Speaker's Advisory Group on Russia, established by the Republican Policy Committee of the U.S. House of Representatives. He has written extensively for major newspapers and journals, and is a frequent commentator in national media. Mr. Saunders is the author of works including *Extended Deterrence in a Changing Asia*, *Russian Energy and European Security*, and *Russia and the Greater Middle East: Challenges and Opportunities* (with Geoffrey Kemp).

Daniel Serwer is a professor at the Johns Hopkins University School of Advanced International Studies, as well as a Senior Fellow at the Center for Transatlantic Relations and a Scholar at the Middle East Institute.

Previously he served as Vice President of the Centers of Innovation at the United States Institute of Peace, where he was Executive Director of the Iraq Study Group, inter alia. He has served as Minister-Counselor at the Department of State and as Special Envoy and Coordinator for the Bosnian Federation, where he negotiated the first agreement reached at the Dayton peace talks. From 1990 to 1993, he was Deputy Chief of Mission and Chargé d'Affaires at the U.S. Embassy in Rome.

Daniel Serwer is the author of various publications, including *Righting the Balance: How You Can Help Protect America*, Potomac Books, November 2013. He blogs at www.peacefare.net and tweets @DanielSerwer.

The opinions expressed in this book are entirely of the authors and do not necessarily reflect those of any institution or government.

András Simonyi is the Managing Director of the Center for Transatlantic Relations at SAIS Johns Hopkins University in Washington DC. He is an economist by training and a former Hungarian Ambassador to the United States and to NATO.

He has been a strong proponent for a smarter combination of Hard and Soft Power tools in the diplomatic/foreign policy toolbox of democracies. He is also an advocate for the strengthening of democratic institutions, of human rights, transparency and accountability, the rule of law as the important aspect of the resilience of societies.

Ambassador Simonyi writes regularly in the *Huffington Post* and other media outlets.

He has his own rock band, the "Coalition of the Willing" in which he plays the electric guitar.

Judit Trunkos is a fourth year PhD student at the University of South Carolina with the first field of International Relations and second field of Comparative Politics. Trunkos has been researching Soft Power, more specifically globalization's influence on Soft Power and Foreign Policy. Trunkos has been working on various methods to compare the different political cultures' influence on the democratization of the selected European countries.

Tom C. Wang is the Deputy Director of the Center for Science Diplomacy of the American Association for the Advancement of Science (AAAS), the world's largest general scientific society, and Executive Editor of its new quarterly publication, Science & Diplomacy (www.sciencediplomacy.org). He also serves as the Director for International Cooperation at AAAS.

Dr. Wang has previously served in the U.S. Department of State's Bureau of East Asian and Pacific Affairs as a science policy adviser. Prior to federal government service, his scientific career included research and engineering positions at Johnson & Johnson and Hewlett-Packard. He received his master's and doctorate degrees in chemical engineering from the Massachusetts Institute of Technology (MIT), and he is a graduate of the University of California at Berkeley with degrees in chemical engineering and political science. He is a term member of the Council on Foreign Relations.

E-mail: twang@aaas.org

The opinions expressed in this book are entirely of the authors and do not necessarily reflect those of any institution or government.